# A JOURNAL BY
## THOMAS HUGHES

**KENNIKAT AMERICAN BICENTENNIAL SERIES**
Under the General Editorial Supervision of
Dr. Ralph Adams Brown
*Professor of History, State University of New York*

A Journal by Thos. Hughes,

for His Amusement.

and

Designd only for His Perusal,

By the Time He attains the Age of 50, if He lives so long.

1778

Begun at York from [illegible]

Having unfortunately lost my First Journal on the retreat 1777, I shall just recapitulate the Heads of what happend to me before that Period, as it occurs to my Memory.—

In the Summer of the Year 1774 was taken from Eton School, and embark'd from Bristol, with my Mother and Family for Ireland. after a Short Passage we [crossed out] landed at Dublin and joined my Father who was Garrison'd there with His Regt. 53: There by being always amongst the Military, I grew enamour'd of a Red Coat; and being allow'd by my Parents to choose my own Plan of Life, I fix'd on the Military Profession, and immediately enter'd as a Volunteer in the 53 Regt (at the Races) in Hopes as I was the only Gentleman amongst six Regiments (then station'd there) in that Capacity, to get an Ensigncy for nothing, I accordingly was introduced by my Friends to the Lord Lieutenant (Lord Harcourt) in my Volunteer Uniform. His Lordship testified His approbation, at seeing a Young Gentleman in that Dress, but though several Vacancies happend about that Time, He did not think proper to appoint me to any, notwithstanding my Plea being backed by near thirty Years Military Service of my Father, after wasting a good deal of Time in vain, and their appearing no prospect of Success from that Quarter, My Friends determin'd to purchase for me, and a Gentleman selling out of my Father's Regt. on Account of His ill state of Health; 400£ were paid in Nov: 1774 for His Ensigncy, & the Resignation in my Favour given in to the Commanding Officer but by some ungenerous Proceedings of that Gentleman the Comm.

Facsimile of the opening page of the Journal

# A Journal
# by Thos: Hughes

*For his Amusement, & Designed only
for his Perusal by the time he attains
the Age of 50 if he lives so long.*

(1778–1789)

With an Introduction by
E. A. BENIANS, M.A.

KENNIKAT PRESS
Port Washington, N. Y./London

A JOURNAL BY THOMAS HUGHES

First published in 1947
Reissued in 1970 by Kennikat Press
Library of Congress Catalog Card No: 70-120880
ISBN 0-8046-1273-0

Manufactured by Taylor Publishing Company     Dallas, Texas

KENNIKAT AMERICAN BICENTENNIAL SERIES

# CONTENTS

# INTRODUCTION

THOMAS HUGHES, the author of the Journal, was one of four brothers, sons of Major William Hughes and Elizabeth Carlyon, all of whom followed their father into the armed forces of the Crown and in an age of world-wide warfare served their country in East or West. His eldest brother, William Carlyon Hughes, who rose to the rank of general, served in the American War and, later, in the West Indies, dying in 1808 while Governor of Surinam. John Hughes, also, served in America and afterwards in India, and was acting A.D.C. to Colonel Wellesley (later Duke of Wellington) at the capture of Seringapatam. The third brother, Philip, became a Captain in the East India Company's fleet. Thomas left Eton in 1774 at the age of fifteen and enlisted as a volunteer in the 53rd Regiment, in which his father held a commission. Shortly afterwards he was able to purchase an ensigncy and in April 1776 his regiment was despatched to Canada as a reinforcement.

Hostilities in North America had begun in the preceding year and American Independence was proclaimed a few weeks after the reinforcement arrived at Quebec. At the time, Sir Guy Carleton was in command in Canada, with Burgoyne second in command. An American attempt on Canada in the previous autumn had been foiled by Carleton's courageous defence of Quebec, and the opening pages of the Journal describe the fighting on the Canadian frontier in the summer of 1776 with the American army in retreat down the Champlain route. Carleton advanced as far as Crown Point and

# Introduction

then withdrew into winter quarters. For the next year, 1777, an offensive stroke was projected to isolate the New England colonies by a combined movement of the British forces assembled in Canada and New York. Burgoyne returned to England to urge this and was sent back to Canada in the spring to command the northern force. In this expedition Hughes took part. Burgoyne's force was inadequate for its task, and no support reached him from the south. Howe's army was engaged in the capture of Philadelphia and Clinton could do little and did that too late. Burgoyne succeeded in taking Ticonderoga on 6 July, but advanced amidst increasing difficulties, and, after hard fighting in September, finding himself surrounded, he surrendered with the remainder of his force to General Gates at Saratoga on 17 October 1777—one of the turning points in the war.

Ensign Hughes himself was made prisoner on 18 September at Ticonderoga where the 53rd Foot were posted on the line of communications. He was taken to Boston, which he finds 'by no means inferior either in size or buildings to the largest towns in England', and thence to Pepperell, where on 7 November the news of the disaster at Saratoga reached him. His active military career was thus a short one, and a great part of his journal records the monotonous routine of a prisoner's life. Parole was given him in due course and he seems to have enjoyed a good deal of freedom. But occupation was hard to find, and there were days 'capable to make an Englishman hang himself'. 'Of all the situations in life', he writes in 1780, 'that of having no pursuit is the worst.' Most of his time was passed in small towns in Massachusetts and Eastern Pennsylvania (of some of which he gives a detailed description), waiting for an exchange which would enable him to return home. While appreciating the treatment of the officers, he comments severely on the sufferings endured by the men, who were for months confined on a guardship, ill-fed and clothed, and finally marched off in the winter to Virginia. But the American militia seemed not much better off.

Meanwhile he kept his Journal, beginning it a second time at New York in 1778, for his first Journal he lost when made prisoner. It is a diary of personal experiences and observations, of the matters that affected and interested him—the scenes around him, the places through which he passed, the behaviour of fellow prisoners, the daily food and comfort of his quarters, the manners and customs of the people, the aspect of the land and the means of getting about, and the amusements and occupations that brightened the daily routine. The chief interest of the Journal is in the picture he gives of social conditions in the colonies. Unlike the young French nobles who had come to serve on the opposite side in the war, he finds nothing romantic in American equality. Town life and social rank are more attractive to him than the rough and equal conditions of the American settlements. With the colonists he had no sympathy: they were simply rebels, certain in due course to be reduced to submission, and the danger was lest Great Britain should grant them too lenient a peace. He records occasional incidents that illustrate the treatment of the Loyalists, the difficulties of the Americans with their levies, and the discontent caused by the depreciation of the currency, rising taxes and the scarcity of provisions. The Continental troops impress him: 'more of the military in their appearance than I ever conceived American troops had attained.'

# Introduction

All the time he followed with the keenest interest the course
and prospects of the war, and reports the rumours that reached
him and the reactions of the Americans to the changing
fortunes of the struggle. News was uncertain and slow, and
he formed no real appreciation of the significance of events
and never contemplated the possibility of British failure. As
late as October 1779, he writes 'That the Colonies will again
be under the jurisdiction of Great Britain is (in my opinion)
a thing of course'. But the American victory at Saratoga and
the hard-fought battle of Germantown had put an end to the
hesitations of France. In February 1778 a Franco-American
Treaty was concluded and war between Britain and France
promptly broke out. For a time Admiral Howe frustrated the
efforts of the Comte d'Estaing, commanding the French army
and fleet, but in the north the British were now thrown upon
the defensive. The French Alliance, followed by the entry of
Spain and Holland into the war, and the formation of a league
of Neutral Nations in Europe, widened the area of the conflict
and repeatedly threatened British command of the sea, without
which there was no prospect of waging successful war in
America. Moreover, victories produced no lasting result; for
gains could not be held in the face of the general hostility of
the people. New England and the Middle Colonies had been
secure from invasion since 1778, and in 1779 the British
Government transferred the war to the South, where for
a time some successes buoyed up their hopes. To the incidents
of the naval war, and to the ups and downs of the fighting in
the Carolinas between Cornwallis on the one hand and Gates
and Nathaniel Greene on the other, the Journal makes a good
many references.

# Introduction

While the issue in the South still hung in doubt, Hughes received the welcome news that an exchange had been agreed to (7 November 1780), but it was not till 14 June 1781 that he got his passage home, only some four months before the surrender of Cornwallis at Yorktown virtually brought the war to an end. In command of a convoy of British invalids he sailed from Sandy Hook with the Cork fleet of victuallers. He describes his return home and his introduction to the gaiety of English society, for which after years of exile he felt no taste:

For my part I was out of my element. Being naturally of a reserved disposition strongly affected by the mauvaise honte, owing to a natural bashfulness and want of good company, I could find little pleasure in a concourse of people whose only amusement was the exhibition of their sweet persons and a laborious attendance on the toilette.

To live in London or Brighton was equally unattractive. So to fulfil a longstanding desire to learn French, and to restore his health, he visited Boulogne:

Here I led the life best suited to my inclination, and which I can look back on with pleasure; there was tranquillity without insipidity, cheerful but not riotous. The morning was dedicated to study and the evening to amusement.

A list of 'a few good books', standard French authors, Molière, Raynal, Voltaire, but not Rousseau, written on the first page of the Journal, suggests the direction of his study. At Boulogne, in January 1784, he received the news of the Peace 'by which America was declared Independent by Great Britain, who lost by the war her blood, her treasure and an empire, owing to a cursed faction and weak ministers'.

## Introduction

His leave expiring, he returned to England, thinking of an exchange to an East India Regiment, when there came 'a thundering order from the War Office against all absent officers'. His regiment was still in Canada, and, glad to exchange an idle existence for military duties again, in September 1784 he rejoined it at Quebec. The latter part of the Journal describes his experiences in Canada—on garrison duty in Quebec and on more active service on the frontier posts. This part of the Journal is written with greater animation and there is a vivid description of the journey up the St Lawrence from Montreal to Detroit, made in twenty-two days, 'the most expeditious', he was told, 'for a number of men that ever was known'. Detroit was the distributing centre of the fur trade and the strategic military position of the West. Of the serious international question involved in the British retention of these fortified trading posts so long after the Peace, Hughes shows no consciousness and perhaps had no knowledge. They controlled the navigation of the St Lawrence and the points of entry to the Great Lakes. All lay in American territory, as defined in the Peace, but had been retained by the British who were concerned to prevent an Indian war and to preserve their monopoly of the fur trade. A ground for this breach of the Treaty was found in the failure of Congress on its side to fulfil its engagements, particularly in regard to the Loyalists. The posts were finally handed over under the terms of Jay's Treaty of 1794. Hughes gives some illustrations of the fierce frontier warfare which raged between the Indians and the Americans, but he never enters upon larger political questions. His description of winter life, both at Quebec and Detroit, and of the progress of the Loyalist settlements through which he passed, is particularly interesting. Hughes had pined in captivity: but he shows his mettle on service, and at Detroit he was both Engineer and Acting Chaplain. The combination of duties seems not inappropriate to the disposition he reveals. The Journal ends with a description of the Indians as he had seen them in the neighbourhood of Detroit, and with the failure of his health. His last entry is dated 23 July 1789. Another hand records his death of consumption on 10 January 1790.

Hughes had begun the Journal as a boy of eighteen and completed it in his thirtieth year. He wrote it, he says, for his own amusement and perusal, and hence the simple directness which is its chief charm. A young officer, with opinions typical of his class and station, of warm family affections and retiring disposition, proud of his profession and of the good name of England, he was one of the multitude of unknown soldiers who in that age gave to king and country good service, ungrudging and unquestioning. He had no part in important affairs, but this unadorned record of his daily life and experience—in time of war, as a prisoner, and, later, serving on the Canadian frontier—with its occasional glimpses of more important figures, though adding little to historical knowledge, has an interest of its own and fills out the picture of the time, giving realism to military life on the outposts of empire in the eighteenth century.

The manuscript, which has been in the possession of his family, has not previously been printed, and is written in a small folio volume on stout unruled paper in a clear hand that grows more mature with the passing of the years. Writing for his own pleasure, the author has made such free use of

# Introduction

abbreviations and followed so individual a system of punctuation and spelling that considerable editorial correction has been necessary for the Journal to be read with ease. This work has been done by Mr R. W. David of the University Press, who has modernised the punctuation and the use of capital letters and corrected the spelling in accordance with Johnson's Dictionary. Some footnotes are given, where necessary for the identification of persons and places and of allusions to the war. In these we have collaborated, and Mr David has supplied the map.

E.A.B.

# A JOURNAL BY THOS HUGHES

for his Amusement

and

Designed only for his Perusal

by the time he attains the Age of 50, if he lives so long

❧

## 1778

### *Begun at New York from Detach'd Papers*

Having unfortunately lost my first Journal on the 18 Sept: 1777 I shall just recapitulate the heads of what happened to me before that period, as it occurs to my memory.

In the summer of the year 1774 was taken from Eaton School, and embark'd from Bristol, with my Mother and family for Ireland. After a short passage landed at Dublin, and joined my Father who was garrison'd there with his Regt, 53rd.[1] Here by being always amongst the military, I grew enamour'd of a red coat, and being allow'd by my Parents to choose my own plan of life, I fix'd on the military profession, and immediately enter'd as a Volunteer in the 53rd Regt (at the age of 15) in hopes, as I was the only gentleman amongst six Regiments (then station'd there), in that capacity to get an Ensigncy for nothing. I accordingly was introduced by my friends to the Lord Lieutenant (Lord Harcourt)[2] in my Volunteer uniform; his Lordship testified his approbation at seeing a young gentleman in that dress, but though several vacancies happened about that time, he did not think proper

---

[1] In 1769 the Irish Establishment had been substantially increased.
[2] Simon, first Earl Harcourt, Lord Lieutenant of Ireland, 1772–7.

to appoint me to any, notwithstanding my plea being back'd by near thirty years military service of my Father. After wasting a good deal of time in vain, and there appearing no prospect of success from that quarter, my friends determin'd to purchase for me, and a gentleman selling out of my Father's Regt on account of his ill state of health, 400£ were lodg'd in Novr 1774 for his Ensigncy, and the resignation in my favour given in to the Commanding Officer; but by some ungenerous proceedings of that gentleman, the commissions were kept back, to procure (as it afterwards appear'd) his son an Ensigncy in the Regt before me, by which means I lost six months pay, and rank; and had two young officers put over my head. My first commission was dated 24th of May 1775; the officer from whom I purchas'd was dead before that time, but luckily for his friends it was not discover'd.

In the spring 1775 the Regt being order'd to Cork, our family remov'd with it. At Cork I was so unfortunate as to lose an affectionate and dear sister, aged 18; she died on the 22nd of December 1775 of a nervous fever, and delirium, occasion'd by the influenza, which raged at that time in every part of Ireland.

On the 4th of April 1776 our Regt, who were then at Kinsale, march'd from thence to Monkstown, and embark'd for America, being part of a reinforcement of 4000 men, destined for Canada,[1] which at that time was thought to be in

---

[1] After the battle of Bunker Hill (17 June 1775) Congress decided to attempt the conquest of Canada, potentially the main British base. A double invasion, by way of Lake Champlain and through Maine, was launched, under Generals Montgomery and Arnold, in the autumn of 1775. The greater part of Canada was rapidly overrun, but the defence of the key-point, Quebec, by Sir Guy Carleton checked the invasion. The American army was still outside Quebec when the reinforcements arrived.

possession of the rebels. My Mother and family remain'd at Cork with an intention of returning to England, the first favourable opportunity, which soon after our departure she perform'd, and took a house in London.

On the 8th of April 1776 my Father, and myself, sail'd from the Cove of Cork, in company with forty transports and two frigates (our convoy). We had a pleasant voyage to the Banks of Newfoundland, where I first saw mountains of ice which I had before read of, but thought it the mere stories of travellers. One of these mountains was so large and high, that our largest ships near it appear'd like boats, and the tops of their masts did not reach a tenth part to the summit. On approaching the Island of Newfoundland we were troubled with fogs, in one of which by mistaking a signal we lost the Fleet, and were for some days alone and in fear of being taken by the American privateers as we carried no guns and the ship was a bad sailor; but, fortunately for us, we fell in with another Fleet, carrying four thousand German troops,[1] under Genl Burgoyne, who had sailed from Portsmouth, about the time of our leaving Cork, and were likewise bound to Canada. With these we continued and enter'd the St Lawrence. The navigation of this river is dangerous, after you pass the Isle of Bic, about 70 leagues from the mouth, but happily our ships met with few accidents, and arriv'd the latter end of May at Quebec. We found all our Fleet from Cork safe; they had arriv'd a few days before and were glad to see us, as it had been reported that we were lost. At Quebec we were not permitted to land, but receiv'd orders to proceed up the river as fast as

[1] The war was unpopular in England and recruiting slow, and to raise the large army required, it was thought necessary to supplement the British forces with a considerable body of hired German troops, chiefly Hessians.

possible, in hopes of cutting off some of the rebels, who were retreating with the utmost expedition.

By the accounts we receiv'd, we found that the Americans after having possession of every other part of Canada had undertaken the siege of Quebec; but it was so vigorously defended by Sir Guy Carleton, and a motley crew of soldiers, sailors, and inhabitants, that all their attempts were frustrated, and in a general attack made by them, under favour of a snow storm on the 31st of December 1775, they were repuls'd with loss, and their favourite general, Montgomery, was left amongst the slain. Notwithstanding this severe check, and the rigours of a Canada winter, they persisted in their endeavours, and blockaded the town so closely, that had not an early arrival of troops prevented their future operations, it was imagin'd the town would have been in the greatest danger of falling into their hands.

From Quebec we proceeded but slowly up the river, on account of the rapidity of the stream and the difficulties of the channel, but our tediousness of sailing was greatly alleviated by the variety of beautiful scenes which upon every bend of the river the country presented to us. To give an idea of the landscapes we saw, a person must conceive a fleet of ships sailing up a large river, in some places scarcely a mile across, in others expanded to 7 or 8, the banks cover'd with farms, houses, villages and churches, except in those few places where precipices rise perpendicular from the river, cover'd with trees in their gayest livery, betwixt which you would often see the foaming silvery cascade; the river in some places interspers'd with woody islands, and winding, so that the ships appear'd at a distance sailing on the land, in others the river stretched as far as the eye could carry; the back ground was generally thick wood with here and there a gentle swell. Such were our enchanting prospects and which, upon our near approach to the shore, were often heighten'd by the view of 5 or 600 soldiers marching in different divisions, on the banks, in martial pomp.

It was the 9th of June when we reacht Trois Rivières about 30 leagues from Quebec. Early in the morning of this day, about 1500 rebels, under a Genl Thompson, attack'd our troops at this place; they came to surprise, but were themselves surpris'd, and defeated, with the loss of their Genl and 500 or 600 men taken or kill'd. They imagin'd there were but 300 men in the town, whereas near 1500 were posted to receive them, their march having been discover'd.

June 11th most of the army having arriv'd, all (but the Light Corps who march'd by land) embark'd again, and proceeded up the St Lawrence to Sorel River. Here the Grenadiers and other Corps disembark'd and pursued the rebels that route, whilst the rest of the fleet continued their way up the St Lawrence with an intention, if the wind had continued favourable, to have got up as high as Longueuil, landed, and cross'd to Chambly, or St Johns, and cut off the rebels' retreat; but the wind and our plan fail'd together, and the rebels made good their escape across Lake Champlain, after having burnt the forts of St Johns and Chambly. The want of boats and vessels prevented our following them, and most of the army, whilst these were preparing, retir'd to cantonments; our Regt was station'd at Iberville on the river Sorel.

Most of the summer was spent in making bateaux for transporting troops, and in procuring a sufficient number of arm'd vessels to drive the rebels out of Lake Champlain, without the command of which it would have been impossible to have carry'd on our operations, intended against Ticonderoga,[1] where the Americans had collected a large body of troops. During this period the troops were train'd to the exercise calculated for the woody country of America, with which they were totally unacquainted; the forts that were destroy'd were rebuilt, and the Province began again to wear the face of government and regularity which the anarchy and confusion introduced by the rebels had depriv'd them of.

About the middle of November our fleet sail'd from St Johns in quest of the rebels. It consisted of one ship of 18 guns, two brigs of 16 and 14, a large radeau, mounting heavy cannon, and near 30 boats, strongly built, and each carrying a great gun in its prow. The Americans had about 17 sail of brigs, galleys, and sloops, from 6, to 16 guns, each. The fleets met; the first engagement was indecisive, yet prov'd our superiority; in the second, the rebels fled, but only 3 vessels escap'd, the rest were burnt, or taken. The lake being in our possession, Sir Guy Carleton with the advance of the army took post at Crown Point, which was abandon'd, but the season being too far spent, he soon return'd, and the troops were put into winter quarters. The part of the Regt I belong'd to. winter'd at Chambly.

---

[1] Lake George and Lake Champlain, together with the Richelieu, or Sorel River, flowing thence into the St Lawrence, afford a convenient pass from the New England States into Canada. The French, when defending Canada against the British, had strengthened it with a chain of forts. Ticonderoga, the most important, had, during the Seven Years' War, withstood all British attempts to force the passage, and was only abandoned to Amherst in 1759, in the final French retreat. Its capture, together with the supporting forts of Crown Point and St Johns, in the spring of 1775, by a small American raiding party, under Ethan Allen and Benedict Arnold, was the prelude to the American invasion of Canada that autumn.

During the winter, which the Canadians said was a very mild one (for my part I thought it cold enough), nothing extraordinary happen'd. We amused ourselves with carrioling. The Carriole is form'd in the body like a one horse chair, with a seat in front for the driver; but instead of wheels it is supported by two pieces of timber shod with iron. It is only us'd on the ice or snow, is drawn by one or two horses, goes very expeditious, and is the easiest mode of travelling I ever experienc'd. The travellers, as they are entirely expos'd to the weather, are always so wrapt in furs, that you often pass intimate friends without knowing each other.

In April three German drafts of our Regt were shot for desertion at the head of the Colours, which being eldest Ensign I carried.

The frost being entirely broke up by May, our Regt, which for the more commodious quartering had been divided, was collected at Chambly. About this time we found that Genl Burgoyne[1] (and not Carleton) was to command the army out of Canada; the latter end of this month, or the beginning of June, the troops intended for the expedition remov'd from the different parts of Canada where they had wintered towards St Johns.

The 4th of June we arriv'd at St Johns, a few days after embark'd in bateaux, and in three days were at Cumberland Head, the place of rendezvous for the army. We remain'd here about a fortnight, and were all inspected by the Genl, from whom we receiv'd the extraordinary order that the army was not to retreat. The whole remov'd from Cumberland Head, and after one or two short stays at different places, landed at, or near, Crown Point and encamp'd.

[1] Carleton was superseded by Burgoyne for the campaign of 1777.

Crown Point is generally reckon'd the head of Lake Champlain, though a large branch, call'd South Bay, runs 50 miles farther up, and on this it is that Ticonderoga lies, where the rebels were posted and as we heard strongly entrench'd. There are the remains of a large French fort and several smaller ones at Crown Point, which I imagine might be made a strong post being on three sides environ'd by water.

Our stay here was as short as could be suppos'd for the purposes of bringing from Canada the different stores for our subsistence, and for carrying on the siege we expected.

I think it was the first of July that the army mov'd in a body up the South Bay, being cover'd by our arm'd vessels which were advanc'd before us. On the same day the whole disembark'd, the Germans on the eastern, and we British on the western shore, making in the whole about 7000 regular, and 1000 irregular troops consisting of Canadians, Indians, and Rangers.[1]

We landed under 3 Mile Point (so called, for being about that distance from Ticonderoga), and the ships were moor'd across the bay, or river, for the protection of the boats, and to keep up the communication between the right and left wings.

Our camp was form'd near the place we landed, in a thick wood which we were oblig'd to clear before we could pitch our tents.

We remain'd here three days, during which proper roads were cut for the troops, to march through the wood, which was thick, and in several places swamps. Our Indians and Rangers were not inactive, as they had several small skirmishes

[1] Many Loyalists were forced to leave their homes and take refuge in Canada. Some went to Chambly, others to Niagara. Here a band of Irregulars, known as the Rangers, was formed by Colonel John Butler.

with the enemy in withdrawing their advanc'd posts; in one of which Lieut Houghton, of our Regt, who acted with the Indians, was wounded.

On the 4th we march'd and took our posts for investing the enemy. We encamp'd on a heighth within about 1000 yards in a direct line from the enemy's works, which were call'd the French Lines (being, as I imagine, the place the French had theirs at the defeat of Abercrombie).[1] Most of our line was cover'd by a thick swampy wood in front, but the rebels soon found us out, and we had scarcely pitch'd our tents before they began a cannonade with six pounders which kill'd a few men, and most of the troops were order'd to encamp farther back, which was soon done, and by retiring 100 yards found security, being cover'd by the hill.

On the 5th our light troops took possession of Sugar-loaf Hill, which entirely overlooks and commands Ticonderoga, and its dependencies, though at a good distance. On this it was intended to have rais'd a battery of heavy cannon, and mortars, which would have annoy'd the enemy greatly; but the rebels prevented our further operation by evacuating their forts early in the morning of the sixth, and retreating, one party by water, up the South Bay, and the rest by land towards Castletown. Had they remain'd twelve hours longer, their escape would have been impracticable, as the Germans that morning were to have been posted on their only remaining communication with the country, and completed their investment. Their retreat was so precipitate that they left not only their public stores and heavy baggage but many of them forgot to take their money and other things of the lightest carriage.

[1] James Abercrombie commanded the unsuccessful attack on the French at Ticonderoga in 1758.

The attainment of this post so easily we thought at that time a presage of future success; but the end prov'd us but shallow politicians, for had this garrison been taken, it is probable there would not have been an army capable of opposing Burgoyne's march to Albany, much less to oblige him and his troops to surrender.

Our surprise was not a little to find about 6 o'clock on the 6th of July that our enemies had given us the slip, but no time was lost in the pursuit; our Grenadiers, Light Infantry &c under Genl Fraser pursued those who went by land, came up with them next day and after a sharp conflict defeated them with loss on both sides, but theirs by far the greatest. This engagement did our troops the greater honour, as the enemy were vastly superior in numbers, and it was perform'd in a thick wood, in the very style that the Americans think themselves superior to regular troops. Whilst this was transacting on shore, the main body of the army (after leaving a strong garrison at Ticonderoga) embark'd, and with our arm'd vessels pusht up the South Bay after the rebels in boats, and 4 or 5 arm'd galleys, that were still remaining from their shatter'd fleet. In the even of the 6th our gun boats came up with them at Skenesborough, attack'd their vessels, took two, and the rest with most of the boats the rebels burnt themselves. The troops landed at Skenesborough the next day; here we found the remains of a fort and some mills burnt by the enemy, who were retir'd to Fort Anne, where on account of bad roads and other impediments it was not thought proper to dislodge them, but a part of the 9th Regt was detach'd to watch their motions.

On the 9th of July our Regt and ⟨the⟩ 47th were order'd to march and bring off the 9th Regt who were attack'd by a very superior body of the enemy and was said to be in great danger of being all taken. We effected our purpose and return'd; the rebels fearing an attack burnt Fort Anne and retir'd further to Fort Edward.

Our long stay at Skenesborough, to make a bad road (scarcely passable) fit for carts &c, and in procuring a sufficient quantity of carriages &c &c for our movement, which by mismanagement came across Lake Champlain slowly and very irregularly, was a primary cause of the miscarriage of Burgoyne's Expedition. During this unfortunate period, gun boats and bateaux were carried across the land from Lake Champlain into Lake George about 1 mile and ½ portage, and some troops from Ticonderoga took post at Fort George, at the Head of that lake, from whence a good waggon road proceeds directly to Fort Edward, distant about 14 miles. The reason, why the main army did not take this route, and to have only sent our light troops, with Indians and Canadians by Skenesborough, is not readily to be defin'd. I suppose it was occasion'd by misrepresentation of the country.

By slow movements we reacht Fort Edward, the rebels retiring leisurely before us. At this place our Regt was order'd to return to Ticonderoga as our Commanding Officer was appointed Governor of that post. About the middle of August we parted from the Army (very much displeas'd at being sent back), and the first day reacht Fort George where we left a garrison; the next morning the rest of the Regt embark'd, and in a day and a half crost Lake George and landed within 2 miles of Ticonderoga—we reliev'd the 62nd who join'd the Army. Here we were again divided, two companies going into Ticonderoga, and the remainder staying at the landing, Lake George, to guard about 100 prisoners, and forward stores. I was unfortunately station'd here.

# The Journal of Thomas Hughes

Soon after this, our communication with Burgoyne's army was destroy'd, on account of his advance, and rebels taking post behind him; however, we heard of the Bennington[1] defeat by some runaway Indians. The return of the Indians we thought then a bad omen, as they seldom leave a victorious army, staying if it is only for the sake of plunder. Nothing happened after this till the 18th of Sept; only that the prisoners and their guard were remov'd from the landing, Lake George, to the landing, Lake Champlain, 1 mile and ½ nearer the French Lines, aliter Ticonderoga.

*18th of September*, 1777. Surprised by a party of 600 men, under a Col: Brown. The enemy attack'd us by daybreak, being so far favour'd by a fog that they had surrounded, and got amongst our marquees by the time they were discover'd. The first thing that alarm'd me was their firing, which was return'd by a sergeant and twelve men (our guard over the prisoners), but they being immediately overpower'd and our communication with each other cut off, no further resistance could be made. We were taken just as you enter the plain that leads to the French Lines after having pass'd the bridge at the saw mills; our numbers were, one captain (Baird), one lieutenant (Gordon), one ensign (Hughes), and 50 privates, but they were so ill of the ague, that we had not 25 fit for duty. One of our men was kill'd and two were slightly wounded. I can lay no blame upon any for this unfortunate event, as we had taken all the precaution that people could in our situation. Our surprise was chiefly owing to the

[1] To protect his line of advance Burgoyne detached two flanking forces to east and west. The eastern force, composed largely of Germans, attempted to raid an American supply depot at Bennington and was decisively defeated by the American commander Stark.

mistake of a sentinel, belonging to a corpl and three men, station'd at the bridge, over which they pass'd. This man had permitted a small party of rebels to approach too near, mistaking them, as he says, for Canadians (a great number of them being there to transport provision over the carrying place); the rebels immediately seized on the sentinel and guard, and then surrounded our post without discovery.

As soon as taken we were carried to a barn at Lake George landing, where they had taken by surprise another detachment of our Regt of the same numbers as ourselves. Here we had time for recollection, hitherto all had been confusion. In this very barn had I often been guard to the Americans, now, sad reverse, those former prisoners with our own weapons prevented my getting out. For about two hours we kept silence, all too much occupied with their own reflections to think of others, though our friends and in the same predicament. At length we were rous'd from our own feelings by the entrance of Lieutenant Lord and 20 men, who had been station'd at an abatised block house for the defence of a saw mill; it seems he had been prepared for them. His sentinel having observ'd a number of men (the party that attack'd us), and the firing afterwards, confirmed the suspicion of their being enemies. Lt Lord had defended himself till the rebels brought a six pounder against him, on which he surrender'd. In the afternoon, the officers and men were separated and sent off under two distinct guards towards Skenesborough. What we could carry on our backs was allow'd us, but not being permitted to return to the place my baggage was, I contented myself with what was brought me by Lt Gordon (who had leave) and by some of our women; these things my men desir'd to carry for me, and I distributed amongst them, and I am happy to say they were all so honest, that I collected them all after two weeks march through the country. About two o'clock we began our march, but as our route lay over mountains, and no particular path, our conductor (who had intended to have brought us to a spring) on its growing dark lost his way, and we stopt on the top of the mountain and were obliged to put up with a bed of rocks. I think I never pass'd such a night, and God forbid I ever should again; cloudy, dark—heavens were my canopy, rocks and stones my bed, my body fatigued and spent with a rough disagreeable march, and not a drop of water, to quench a burning thirst occasion'd by perspiration; the wind whistled, and portended a storm, interrupted now and then by the challenge of my enemies who surrounded me, or by the distant, solemn sound of the cannons which were fired during the night from Fort Independence.

We march'd at daybreak Sept 19 by a road pass'd but once before. In many places the mountains were so steep, we were obliged to pull ourselves up, and let ourselves down by the branches of the trees. About ten o'clock, to our great joy, we reacht a small stream of water on the sides of which were a number of huts, or rather what the Indians call wigwams; this was the place they lay, two nights before they took us. We remain'd here two or three hours, to dress some provision, then reassum'd our march, and about 4 o'clock arriv'd at South Bay, the place of their crossing. Here we found two or three boats under a guard. Our soldiers being all sent across, the officers and servants were put into a boat, which carried us to Skenesborough in 6 hours. A room in Col: Skene's house was given to the officers in which was a woman and 3 children ill of the small pox, one of whom died during the night; the poor woman's lamenting her son disturb'd us, but she being remov'd, I never rested better, being fatigued.

SEPT: 20TH. On awaking this morning we found the room full of Yankee soldiers who had come out of curiosity to view the regulars, as they call'd us; but they were soon driven out by order of the Commanding Officer, who posted two sentinels at our door, to prevent their further intrusion. After which the same person sent us some chocolate for breakfast. This being finish'd and we just departing, a man accosted us (by announcing himself Waiter to the Col: commanding the troops) and said his master would be oblig'd to any of us for a shirt or two, and that as we were going down the country by calling at the Col's house we might get the like number from his wife. But in doing this we all beg'd to be excus'd, as in the first place we did not know his place of abode, and if we had, it would have been much against us, our passing it; but indeed our real reason of refusal was all of us having so few we had none to spare. March'd to Castletown; they gave us two rooms and a good allowance of fresh provision. Our soldiers who had gone a different way met us here.

SEPT: 21ST. Hir'd horses of our guard and went as far as Pawlet; our road to day was a very curious one, as we just entered what is call'd the Green Mountains. These mountains here do not run in ridges as they do farther down but rise up generally singly to a great heighth and of a variety of forms. Our way lay round the bottoms of these steep rocks and was so very crooked that we seldom saw 300 yards before us. The Col: who commanded at Pawlet treated us with great civility, but for want of conveniencies the head of an old barrel stood us in place of dishes and plates and our fingers of knives and forks.

SEPT: 22ND. It rain'd a deluge and we remain'd at Pawlet. A report of an engagement between Burgoyne and Gates (who commands the American army); it happen'd on the 19th but we have no particulars.[1]

SEPT: 23RD. Marched to Manchester, where we remain'd for the day. Some of our officers having bought a young bear, we had it dress'd, and it prov'd a great treat, being in taste not unlike veal. The engagement of the 19th was confirm'd; the rebels confess that we kept the field, but that it cost us dear.

SEPT: 24TH. Arriv'd at Bennington. Here we had a parole from Genl Gates which extended to Boston; the purport of it was, that we should go through the country without molesting the inhabitants, or talking of affairs concerning the states, and that we should have a conductor, who was to see that we were treated according to our rank, pay our expenses and deliver us, when we came to Boston, into the hands of the Commissary of Prisoners. After signing this parole, we were sent to the house of a Col: Brush, who treated us with great hospitality. In the afternoon we visited a Mr Salans of the 9th Regt, who lay very ill of a wound he receiv'd in the engagement near this place, in which he was so unfortunate as to be made prisoner; indeed by his account few of our troops escap'd in that action, the whole of the detachment being either kill'd, wounded, or taken. Salans insisted that Brown and me should sleep at his house; this was the more agreeable as we had not taken off our clothes since the morning of our captivity.

SEPT: 25TH. Bennington is the first place that we have met in these back regions that has the least appearance of a town. It consists of a Meeting House (fill'd with wounded

[1] This engagement was the attack on the American fort of Stillwater, which was the limit of Burgoyne's advance.

men) and 12 or 14 dwelling houses. In England it would scarcely be entitled to the name of village, but in this country, every six square miles being a township, you may pass through some towns that has neither houses or inhabitants. This town is situated in the midst of the Green Mountains, and is the metropolis of the State of Vermont, a numerous banditti so call'd,[1] who acknowledge no government, but call themselves allies to the United States. It was a party of Vermonters that took Ticonderoga and Crown Point (at the beginning of these disturbances) and made the garrison prisoners. These owe their independence to the strength of their country, from whence it would be an arduous task to dislodge them. It is surprising what a multitude of militia has pass'd through this since our arrival; they say the lion is caught in the net and talk of Burgoyne's capture as a thing of course.

SEPT: 27TH. Being rather too many for Col: Brush's house, a party of us went to Williamstown; where we are to remain till the others come up.

SEPT: 28TH. Williamstown has fewer houses than Bennington, but the country is less mountainous, and much better clear'd. In sauntering about this morning, I found the vestiges of an old fort, but time had so reduced the earthen ramparts, that I could not trace its form or extent. In a small stream, that wash'd one side, were several pieces of old cannon, which I imagine were flung in there at the demolition.

SEPT: 29TH. After church (this being Sunday) the inhabitants came in crowds to see us, and appear'd surpris'd to find us like themselves. The rest of the gentlemen coming from Bennington under a conductor, we took the opportunity

[1] I.e. the 'Green Mountain Boys'. They provided the party responsible for the capture of Ticonderoga in 1775 (see note on p. 6).

of some horses going down the country and went off this evening. After riding 8 or 9 miles, we were billeted off on the houses by the road. Luckily for me I got into the house of a friend to government, who gave the best his house afforded —and here I cannot help lamenting the deplorable situation of the Loyalists, who because they will not violate their oath of allegiance, by taking the test tendered them by their upstart rulers, are turn'd out of their houses, their estates sold, and themselves and families reduced (some from affluent and all from easy circumstances) to beggary and want. Such is the Land of Liberty! The man in whose house I now am, is only suspected to be what the rebels call a Tory; but on this bare suspicion they have put a man in the house, to live at free quarter (and who in reality is more master than the owner himself), to watch his motions and to give an account of all he says. Liberty! How long wilt thou allow thy name as a cloak to the most abject slavery, and dependence.

SEPT: 30TH. Treated very indifferently on the road and at night had some difficulty to procure a place to lay in, the houses being taken up with American troops; after waiting about two hours in the road with reluctance a room was given us and we all slept on the floor.

OCTOBER 1ST. Went through Northampton, a large well built town, situated in a fine open country near the banks of the river Connecticut; we cross'd this river to a town, called Hadley, a very neat pleasant place consisting of one long and broad street, the buildings very regular, having each a small garden in front. At the upper end of the street (which extends near a mile) stands the Meeting House, built in good taste and has a pretty effect. The country near the banks of the river is well clear'd and thickly settled with towns, villages, and farms;

indeed it has a most picturesque appearance, to us it appeared a paradise, after having been so long involv'd amongst gloomy woods and mountains. The Province of Connecticut is the most fruitful of all the New England states and raises more wheat than all the others put together. After quitting the environs of Hadley, where we dined, we again entered a woody country or, according to the expression of the inhabitants, a wilderness, and arriv'd late in the evening at Amherst, where we were tolerably accommodated.

Ocт: 2ND. At Hardwick—here we have two good inns and, as some of us are a good deal fatigued, our conductor agrees to our staying a day to recruit. One of the inns is kept by a Brig: Genl of the Americans—one Warner.[1]

Ocт: 3RD. The people tell us that we are now out of the wilderness and that we shall have a well inhabited country the rest of our journey. Indeed if it is all like this, it will be much beyond my expectations—the face of the land is not a continued series of open country but every farm has a wood lot which is their only fuel (the striking contrast betwixt these clumps of wood and their till'd and meadowlands forms a beautiful variety). At this time fruit is in such plenty that their hogs are fed on apples, peaches and chestnuts.

Ocт: 4TH. Horses being difficult to procure, we did not leave Hardwick till after dinner; about 9 at night reacht Rutland, and were treated with the utmost civility.

Ocт: 5TH. Being Sunday we met numbers of people on the road, and at the inn (we breakfasted) found a large party of militia singing psalms. The tavern at Marlborough where we put up for the even is not kept by the civilest people; at first they refus'd us every thing because we were Britons; but what

[1] Seth Warner commanded a battalion of the Green Mountain Boys.

with a little entreaty on our part, back'd with some threats from our conductor, they allow'd us to enter, and we fared better than could be expected.

OCT: 6TH. Past through two or three small towns, at one of which we found our poor fellows, the soldiers taken with us. Their route had been entirely different from ours and so had their treatment, they having been oblig'd to march sometimes two days without provision, and when they receiv'd it, the allowance was not half sufficient; and they all protested that were it not for the fruit they gathered on their march, they must have died of hunger. My servant collected all my necessaries from them, which had been given on the 18th of September. About 4 o'clock arriv'd at Boston; we entered by the Neck, on which the remains of our works are still visible. The lines of the Americans at Roxborough are preserv'd entire; they do not appear very strong. Our first business here was waiting on the Commissary of Prisoners who call'd us a parcel of cut-throat rascals, and ordered us instantly on board the Guard-ship. His passion being a little moderated, he condescended, at last, to allow us to remain in Boston for this night, provided we pay our own bill; but that on tomorrow we should go on board the Guard-ship. Matters being thus settled, some of us thought proper to see the town; but our walk was soon interrupted by an express from one Genl Heath who ordered us to remain at our inn, as the inhabitants were not pleased with seeing those who had murdered their friends. Boston, by the little we saw, is by no means inferior either in size, or buildings, to the largest towns in England. It stands on a peninsula, jutting out at the bottom of a commodious harbour, and is joined to the Continent by a low sandy strip of land, commonly call'd the Neck. Before these unhappy disputes it carried on a most extensive trade, but I believe now that they have few or no imports except prize goods; and those cannot be a great quantity as I observ'd most of their shops shut.

OCT: 7TH. With a parcel of Commissaries in front, and a number of vagabonds at our heels, we were paraded through the town and put on board a ship design'd for our prison. The 7 officers of our Regt were crowded into a hole, honour'd with the name of Cabin (hardly large enough to swing a cat), without bedding, knives, forks, plates, or the least conveniencies, no person allow'd to come to us, and none of us permitted to go on shore and provide anything; as an addition to our distress, every crevice is full of vermin. There are two hundred other prisoners (with countenances the pictures of famine) in the hold of the ship. They are separated from us by a high barricade which runs across by the main mast; amongst these are some of our Regt taken at Bennington. The only consolation we have is that our overseer, or Captain, appears civil, and promises to make it as little disagreeable as our situation will admit.

OCT: 8TH. Receiv'd a letter from Genl Heath, in which he informs us of the quantity of provision allow'd. It is sufficient for people in our situation as we can take little exercise. This Heath is a person of mean extraction, and was, at the commencement of this rebellion, a brick-layer.

OCT: 9TH. Our only amusement is the prospect, which is extensive; on one side lies the town of Boston; on the other Bunker Hill,[1] with all the heights on which Washington

[1] Boston was the chief commercial centre in America, and the scene of the first repressive measures. After the battle of Bunker Hill Gage found himself hemmed in by enormously superior forces, and his successor, Sir William Howe, evacuated the town in March 1776.

rais'd forts, whilst Boston was in our possession. We are moored about 100 fathom from the shore, near Beacon Hill, above Charlestown Ferry—there is another prison ship within 200 yards of ours fill'd with sailors, but none of us are permitted to go on board each other.

OCT: 10TH. Some of the prisoners laid a plot for seizing the ship, binding the Yankees on board, and making their escape in the long boat; this night was fixed on for the execution of it, but it being discovered by a Canadian, a strong guard was sent on board, and the ring-leaders put in irons.

OCT: 12TH. To pass off a tedious minute, I shall describe the passing of one day—which will serve for the whole, there being no variety. At 9 o'clock (Arouse is the word) we jump up from the floor, and without the trouble of putting on our clothes, being always dress'd, we fall to our breakfast, consisting of boil'd rice, sprinkled with salt, and garnish'd with a few lumps of stinking butter, to prevent its sticking in the throat. This meal finish'd, we mount the quarter deck, which is almost five paces long; here we amuse ourselves with walking, sitting, and talking about the weather, wind, tide, &c &c till one o'clock, when a servant announces the dinner being ready. Our dinners always (like those of the foundation boys at Eaton) consist of one dish, with this trifling difference—theirs consists of mutton, ours salt pork, with ship biscuit. Our apparatus is first the top of a chest of drawers for table (rather the worse for wear); instead of table cloth, about an inch of grease and dirt. Our plates are form'd of pieces of wood, our dish a wooden bowl; 3 one prong'd forks, and two knives, are laid in order (those that have knives to cut for the rest). Our drink is very small beer (generally sour) and water. After dinner one of the drawers receives the meat, which is laid by for supper. Our afternoon is the most tedious part of the day, so that by 8 o'clock we are heartily tired, when we take a slight repast, and lay down on the floor of the cabin, thicker than three in a bed.

OCT: 15TH. Two of our men made their escape by slipping unobserv'd into the boat, untying, and letting her drive on shore, they laying at the bottom; this exploit was perform'd during a hard shower.

OCT: 17TH. Most of the gentlemen being unwell, Capt: Davies having the fever and ague and myself a violent dysentery, occasion'd by our confined situation and bad diet, we wrote to the Council of Boston and desir'd leave to go into the country on parole.

OCT: 18TH. Our request being granted, a Commissary brought us a parole for the town of Pepperell—but we are limited to a mile.

OCT: 19TH. Our ship remov'd her station and fell down below Charlestown where we came to close along-side another prison-ship, on board of which were all our men taken with us, and the officers of His Majesty's Ship the Fox. We were permitted to breakfast with them—after which we were sent on board a ship full of sailors.

OCT: 20TH. All landed at Charlestown, where both officers and servants were immediately put into one horse chairs—and off we went for Pepperell under the care of a conductor. Lay this night at Concord—22 miles.

OCT: 21ST. Arrived at Pepperell, and were delivered over to the Committee of the town, who distributed us about the neighbourhood for this night. I lay at one Gibson's, who was formerly a cornet in the provincial service, the greatest blackguard, and the greatest rebel, I ever met with.

OCT: 22ND. Procur'd quarters in a house, in which I have agreed to pay two silver dollars pr week for board &c &c. The family are very civil—it consists of Father (who is almost deaf), Mother (a talkative old woman), and two daughters, who are of the order of old maids, confounded ugly, with beards an inch long.

OCT: 25TH. This town is quite a new settlement and so little clear'd that in some places the houses are a mile distant. We are almost as much out of the world here, as if we were in the deserts of Arabia, and the inhabitants as ignorant as the Hottentots. I have been asked how often I have visited Jerusalem and if I did not live close by it, though I told them I lived in England; and then they ask'd, if England was not a fine town. What a life am I to lead? I am sick of their absurdities.

OCT: 26TH. I find that the people here have not the least idea of a gentleman. Our servants are treated just like ourselves, and they are surpris'd to find our men won't eat at the same table with us, to which they are always invited. Two of our gentlemen agreeing with some inhabitant about boarding, the only thing the people objected to, was the article of washing. Oh! if that is the only obstacle (says a Committee man, who went with them) it is easily remov'd; send them a tub, and give them a little soap, and they can wash their own clothes.

NOVEMBER 1ST. This life being such a one as perhaps I may never see again, I cannot refrain describing it. We have but one room to eat and sit in, which is in common with all the family, master, mistress, and servant, and what to call it, I know not, as it serves for parlour, kitchen, and workroom. About 9 o'clock, Lt Brown (who lives with me) and myself breakfast, but they all wonder how we can sleep so long. Our breakfast is bread and milk, or boil'd Indian corn with butter and treacle spread over it. This is pretty substantial, and after it we generally walk into the woods, to gather chestnuts, or throw stones at squirrels. About 12 o'clock the whole family collects for dinner, which soon after smokes upon the board; and whilst it is cooling, Father shuts his eyes, mutters an unintelligible monstrous long grace and down we all sit with no other distinction, but Brown and me getting pewter plates —whereas the others have wooden platters. Our food is fat salt pork, and sauce (the name they give to roots and greens). We never get fresh meat, but when a fox, or hawk, seizes an unfortunate fowl, but being discover'd by the noise we make, is frighten'd, and lets fall the prey, generally with the loss of a leg or wing. The fowl on this disaster is immediately pickt and put into the pot. The dinners are upon that free and easy mode, that neither gentleman or lady use any ceremony—all hands in the dish at once—which gives many pretty opportunities for laughter, as two or three of us often catch hold of the same piece. This meal over, another grace is said, and we all disperse to our different employments, theirs working and ours the best we can find. At night fall a large fire is made on the hearth, and the kitchen (or whatever it is) receives the whole family, which would present an high scene to an unconcern'd spectator—Mother, Brown and me round the fire, she knitting and asking us silly questions; our servant at the opposite corner of the chimney from us; at our back two or three women spinning with large noisy wheels, and in the middle of the room sits Father, and one or two apprentice boys shelling Indian corn. We have no candles, but the room is lighted by splinters of pine wood flung into the fire. About 8 o'clock we get bread and milk for supper; a little after

Father begins to yawn—upon which we stand up. He says prayers, and we depart to our beds. Our apartment, or rather the place we lay in, extends over the whole house, and is what is commonly call'd the garret. We have three beds in it—one of which contains Brown and me, in the second sleep our two young ladies, and close at their feet, in the third, rest the servant and apprentice. Our room is not the worse for being a repository of fruit, and nuts, as we generally make an attack on the apples before we get up of a morn. If this is the kind of life the poets say so much of, and call Rural Happiness, I wish to my soul that they were here, and I in London.

Nov: 7TH. Genl Burgoyne's defeat[1] on the 7th ult: has reach'd us (inhabitants of the wilderness), and the people here will have it that himself, and army, have all surrender'd, and that they are to be march'd to Boston—a bitter pill if true, but I have great hopes it is not, as these New Englanders are much given to humbugging.

Nov: 12TH. Its true, it's pity, and pity it is, it's true. Alas! Unfortunate Burgoyne and still more unfortunate Army. The report is they have surrender'd on terms, one of which is, they are to go to England and not serve in America during the war. That they will not serve in America, I believe the Americans will take care of; but their going to Great Britain does not appear to me so certain.

Nov: 20TH. There is something in the characters of these New Englanders that I cannot illustrate. They are certainly

---

[1] The surrender at Saratoga of Burgoyne's whole surviving force. On account of the terms of surrender, or convention, by which the prisoners were to be allowed to return to England on condition of not serving again in North America during the war, they came to be known as the Convention Army. Congress found a pretext for refusing to fulfil the terms of the agreement.

all very religious, and very industrious—and yet the men are ⊓
not over nice in point of honesty, and loss of virtue amongst
the women does not sully their reputation. I believe they
think different from the rest of the world.

NOV: 29TH. Not having seen each other for some time, we
met to day by appointment, and dined together at a public
house. We were all very merry, but in the end one or two
getting mellow and kicking up a dust, they were sent to
prison, for talking disrespectfully of the Congress,[1] by one
Scott, an Irishman and a captain in the rebel service who was
(by his own confession) oblig'd to leave his country for none
of his good deeds. Baird and Lord are the heroes.

DECEMBER 9TH. An order from the Council of Boston, to
take us all to gaol for exceeding our limits by dining at the
public house; which it seems we had (by almost 150 yards).
The Sheriff took us into custody and, as he had two prisons
under his jurisdiction, was so polite as to offer us the choice
of Concord or Cambridge. We chose the latter as Genl Burgoyne's army are quarter'd there. We lay this even at Lexington.

DEC: 10TH. Our sheriff was so far from taking any care
for preventing an escape that he left us entirely to ourselves,
and upon our arrival we were 3 hours in the town of Cambridge before we could find him; but at last meeting him in
the street, we stopt him. Well, says he, I am a little busy, but
I will settle you first. The prison being near he deliver'd us
to the jailor—with an injunction to use us well. Our keeper
is a civil old fellow, and has given us the best room in his own

---

[1] The first Continental Congress of representatives of the Colonies met
in September 1774; the second met in May 1775 and assumed the
direction of the war.

house—so that we are not in the least confin'd. We have agreed with him to mess us, at the rate of 3 paper or one silver dollar pr day—extravagant enough! but what is to be done? Either submit to this or be put into rooms—the bare sight of which strikes one with horror. Several Convention officers[1] intend messing with us so that we shall make a jolly party.

DEC: 15TH. Plenty of good company—plenty of good eating, and drinking—but devilish shy of cash; if we don't procure money soon, we shall be oblig'd to remain here for debt. An application has been made to Genl Burgoyne for subsistence, but it seems the paymaster is quite dry.

DEC: 18TH. Our old boy begins to talk of payment, his bill is 150 pounds. My only comfort is that it is to be paid in paper money. I begin to think a jailor in America is the same as a jailor all over the world.

DEC: 20TH. Frost bit three of my fingers, but by rubbing them with snow I have almost recovered them again. It is very extraordinary that heat and cold should have the same effect, for my fingers are blistered, and burn as if I had put them in the fire.

DEC: 22ND. The jailor came to us this morning (with a countenance that spoilt my breakfast and foretold what he had to say), which was, all his cash was spent, and he had nothing to go to market with—a lying old dog, his daughter tells me he has 5 or 600 pounds upstairs in his desk. The covetous antiquated fellow is as deaf to all argument as a bailiff executing a writ, though we demonstrate to him, the best in the world, by turning out the inside of our pockets. I do not know what would have been the result of our conference, had not the

---

[1] See note on p. 26.

## December 1777

Earl of Balcarres[1] call'd, who, seeing our situation, gave him ten guineas, and which gave us peace for the day.

DEC: 27TH. This mode of life will never do for my finances. Our mess is after the rate of 14 guineas pr month, which will never agree with 3 shill: and 6 pence pr day. As soon as we can procure cash, which we expect daily, I must abdicate and return (if I cannot go to any place else) to Pepperell, and feed on pork and sauce.

DEC: 29TH. Genl Burgoyne sent word that he intended waiting on us, but for some reasons he has defer'd his visit. Such a number of our friends come to see our quarters, that we call the gaol, the Coffee House.

[1] Lord Balcarres commanded the Light Infantry in Burgoyne's army.

JANUARY 1ST. A very pretty prospect for the opening of a New Year. In gaol, no money, few clothes, and indebted to a considerable amount to the gaoler (the worst man in the world); to counterbalance this, a light heart, thin pr of breeches (in the strictest sense of the word), a good deal of hope, and this comfortable saying—it might have been worse.

JAN: 5TH. Receiv'd money, paid the jailor, who is in good humour again—and wrote to the Council, to get out of his clutches.

JAN: 7TH. The Council sent word, that Lts Brown, Gordon, and Ensn Hughes might return (when they thought proper) to the town of Pepperell. Captain Baird, Davies, and Lord choose to remain where they are

JAN: 9TH. Parted with our friends, and lay this even at Littletown, on our way back to Pepperell. Ld Balcarres inform'd me of my succeeding to a Lieutenancy in the Regt, occasion'd by the death of Capt: Wight of our Grenadier Company, who was kill'd in the engagement of the 9th of October last. I am indebted to His Lordship for this promotion.

JAN: 10TH. Arriv'd at our old quarters—and have procur'd lodging in a much better house than any former. My present landlord is an inn-keeper, head man of the Committee, Representative of the town, and Lieut Col: of the American standing forces. The fellow is a great rebel, but politicks being a topick I make a rule of avoiding, I hope we shall agree.

FEBRUARY 5TH. All got together again, Baird, Lord, and Davies having been taken out of gaol, and sent up here by order of Council. If a quiet life is a blessing, we are certainly happy fellows—oh! for a sleep of three months.

APRIL 18TH. Not agreeing with my landlord, at his request quitted the house and live now in the same house with Capt: Baird. It seems one Mrs Rogers, and a certain Mr Woods (olim, my landlord), threaten to shoot me, but imagine that they will not let their passion get the better of their prudence— so perhaps they will think better of it.

APRIL 28TH. Faith! I wish myself fairly out of this place, for though I have nothing to say to the inhabitants, it is by no means agreeable to be in the power of rascals, who only wait a proper opportunity to murder one.

APRIL 30TH. Some men cutting down a tree, a number of squirrels jumpt out of a hole near the top, and flew away. The oddness of the sight led some of us (who were near) to a pursuit, and we soon caught three. They were of a reddish brown colour—rather smaller than the common ground squirrel, and only differ from them by their having two small thin membranes, growing from the shoulders of their fore legs, and reaching to their hind ones; when they spring to any great distance they extend these kind of sails, which supports them in a descent (for they cannot mount) for twenty or thirty yards.

MAY 8TH. Every thing being in bloom, my entertainment is observing a number of humming birds extracting honey from the peach and cherry blossom; they buzz about like so many bumble bees which at first I took them for. Their shyness, and rapidity of flight, preventing a near view of them, we requested Capt: Davies to try shooting one; which after many fruitless attempts, he at last succeeded in, and kill'd one with sand. This bird was very little bigger than a large drone, of the finest proportion that possibly can be imagin'd—but its plumage beggars description. The back and wings were a fine brown ting'd with purple; the neck display'd such a variety of colours, that it is almost impossible to particularize any— sometimes it was of a golden colour, another direction of a deep green, and in a third light a bright scarlet. The legs (about the size of a pin) and bill of a dark colour; the bill was an inch in length, and so sharp, it enter'd the flesh like a needle. We intended preserving this curiosity—but Madam Grimalkin devour'd it.

MAY 18TH. All remov'd to Concord by order of the Commissary, where we are to remain. Our parole extends over the whole town, which is large and well settled. It was at the north bridge in this town that the 1st American action began—our troops marching from Boston, here, to destroy warlike stores.[1]

MAY 27TH. Two other officers and myself procur'd boarding in the house of a Mrs Bliss—the genteelest woman I have met with in New England. She has four sons—all officers— two in the British, and two in the American service.

JUNE 7TH. Caught the fever and ague; the doctor tells me I have the jaundice—but I do not believe him.

JUNE 9TH. I have a severe fit of the ague every day. I cannot express the obligations due Mrs Bliss and daughter who use me as affectionately as if I was one of their family.

JUNE 24TH. A great eclipse of the sun. Intelligence that Sir Henry Clinton had left Philadelphia and was marching through the Jerseys towards New York.

JUNE 28TH. Intensely hot—and not a breath of air.

---

[1] On 18 April 1775 Gage sent a force to destroy stores at Concord, which suffered severely on its return journey at Lexington. This was the beginning of hostilities.

JUNE 30TH. Great quantities of bark has freed me of the ague. My American doctor has refused every pecuniary reward and behav'd very genteelly.

JULY 5TH. An action happen'd in the Jerseys[1] occasion'd by Washington attempting to stop the progress of our army to New York. Accounts vary with respect to which side victory turn'd, but have strong reason to imagine that the British drub'd them, as the rebels confess our safe arrival at York—but that we escap'd by moonlight.

JULY 16TH. The people are all in high spirits and talk of driving the British off the continent; this is occasion'd by a fleet of French ships having appeared on the coast much superior to our force in these seas. What truth there is in this report time must unfold, but should not be much surpris'd at the confirmation, as we all know that French treaties are kept no longer than when an opportunity offers for them to break them to their advantage.[2]

JULY 28TH. It is but too true that the French Fleet are upon the coast; they consist of 12 ships of the line and 4 frigates and are commanded by one Count D'Estaing, a man notorious for having violated his parole twice last war. By the last

[1] A reference to the action at Monmouth Court House in June 1778. Sir Henry Clinton, who had just succeeded Howe as Commander-in-Chief, was withdrawing the British forces from Philadelphia to New York, with Washington in pursuit. Charles Lee, commanding the American advanced guard, avoided action, and Clinton made good his escape. Washington declared that a decisive opportunity had been lost.

[2] France regarded the Treaty of Paris as a truce rather than as a lasting peace, and, even before the Declaration of Independence, was giving covert help to the Colonists. In February 1778 she recognised the independence of the United States and entered into an alliance with them, hoping also to secure the support of Spain. War between Britain and France promptly followed, and in April the Comte d'Estaing left Toulon with the French Fleet, for North America.

accounts, the French were lying off Sandy Hook, withinside which was Ld Howe[1] with the British Fleet. We expect every day to hear of a naval engagement; the French being so superior will scarcely forgo the opportunity of striking a severe blow before any reinforcement can come out from England.

AUGUST 4TH. The rebels are now determin'd (as they say) to attempt an affair[2] which, if crown'd with success, will go a great way to end the war. Their plan is the taking of Rhode Island. They made a feint against the Island last year, but want of a command in shipping prevented their landing. That obstacle is now remov'd by favour of the French, who are to attack Newport (where our troops are) vigorously by Sea; whilst the Americans, with an army of 30,000 men, carry on regular approaches against our works (which are strong and go quite across the Island). The number of our troops on the Island are 6000. If volunteers for this expedition flock from every quarter, as fast as they do from this, instead of 30,000 they may have an army of 100,000 men.

AUGT 7TH. It not being convenient for Mrs Bliss to board us any longer, as she had no man to hunt after provisions which are scarce, left her house, and live now with a Dr Lee —a great friend to Government.

AUGT 9TH. Extremely pleased with my new house, on account of a Mr Gardener who boards with me. He is a person that has seen most parts of Europe, and has had a good education. Not agreeing in sentiment with these people, he is stigmatis'd with the name of Tory, and though a man of

[1] Earl (Richard) Howe, the admiral, brother of Sir William (later Viscount) Howe, the general.

[2] The plan for joint action against Newport in Rhode Island by d'Estaing and Sullivan was frustrated by Lord Howe, whose prompt action had thus saved in turn the two British bases, New York and Newport.

considerable property they hardly allow him money enough to appear decent. He is more a prisoner than we are and is permitted to remain here on parole for the benefit of his health; I have had several conversations with him on the subject of the war, which he seems to think might have been finish'd some time ago, if the commanders in chief had pusht it with vigour. However he is still positive it must end in our favour, even if we only act on the defensive, as the depreciation of their paper currency must ruin them—we get now 4 paper dollars for one hard or silver one.

AUGT 12TH. We are all now in suspense to see how the Rhode Island expedition turns out; nothing but that is talked of. It is amusing to observe how eager the inhabitants are for news—every traveller is stopt—the crowd gathers—and if a Committee man is amongst them, he assumes an air of consequence, and interrogates the man. By this means we have generally 6 or 7 different reports of a day—and the last is sure to be credited, provided it be but favourable. To day a man was near being sent to gaol, for saying that Adml Byron[1] with a strong squadron from England was on the coast.

AUGT 16TH. The siege is at last begun, and the rebels are so very positive that they shall carry the place that many have gone entirely for the sake of the plunder of Newport, and those that remain at home are already talking of what will be done next. Some are for taking Long Island, but the greatest part are for attacking New York—for by that means (say they) the Philistines will be entirely driven out of the Land of Canaan. How foolish will these Yankees look, should the arm of the Philistines prove too strong for them.

[1] Vice-Admiral John Byron was despatched to the West Indies in pursuit of d'Estaing in June 1778.

The best intelligence I can pick up mentions Count d'Estaing having entered the harbour of Newport, under a severe cannonade from our forts, where he has destroy'd 5 of our frigates, that had not an opportunity of putting to sea. The rebels have advanced their approaches within 700 yards of our advance works.

AUGT 19TH. Certain intelligence that Ld Howe has collected a number of ships, and gone from Sandy Hook, for the relief of Rhode Island. His force is inferior to the French, but what may we not expect from British valour? The Tories, whose spirits were much depress'd on the present situation of affairs, are now reviv'd and laugh at their former fears—and here I must observe, that both Whig and Tory are the same people, being elated beyond bounds with the least shadow of success, and as much depress'd when they apprehend any misfortune approaching. They are a chicken hearted race.

AUGT 27TH. Reports have been so very contradictory for some days past that nothing could be credited. At last truth has emerged (for the sake of putting these rascals to the blush) and show'd us they all lied. Ld Howe appear'd off Newport (sometime last week) with an intention if the Count had remain'd in the harbour to have sent in some fire-ships; but the French man was too cunning—as soon as our Fleet appear'd he slipt his cables and put to sea, our batteries as he pass'd saluting him with such good will that the French acknowledge a good deal of shagreen at not being capable of returning the compliment. On the Count's going out, our Fleet stood out to sea. The French follow'd—the day following the Fleets were near—ours still avoiding the engagement; but in the evening the breeze fresh'ning my Lord lay to with an intention of fighting—as the French on account of the sea

[ 36 ]

could not open their lower ports, the Fleets were on an equality—but the Count now thought proper to decline what before he was so eager for. That night a storm dispers'd the Fleets, and the Count, after losing his masts, and receiving a severe peppering from one of our 50 gun ships who met him in that situation, and would have taken him, if others had not arriv'd to his assistance, is now on his way to Boston, to refit, having only appear'd off Rhode Island. He leaves the honour of taking it to the Americans; what kind of an exit they will make, we shall soon see—the Whigs' faces lengthen amazingly of late.

AUGT 30TH. Those people who, on their march through this town to take Rhode Island, were very merry, and out of their abundant goodness used to call us Lobster-backs, now sculk through the town and want to be unnoticed; but as we are generally on the Green, by which they all pass, we recognize our old friends, and ask them if the Island has surrendered. Their only return is a shake of their head, and a hearty curse on the French, for leaving them in the lurch.

SEPTEMBER 2ND. The important affair is now over and they have made a good retreat from the Island with the loss of 300 men by their accounts. They esteem themselves very happy to have escap'd so well, and believe they will have no inclination to disturb our troops a second time. The action in which they lost these men happen'd on the 29th of Augt, as they were retiring; as usual they made it entirely in their favour and pretend they beat us back with great loss.

SEPT: 4TH. Count d'Estaing has arriv'd at Boston Harbour to refit, and is fortifying some islands at the mouth, for fear Adml Byron (who is certainly on the coast) should attack him.

SEPT: 8TH. Several Navy officers (who were taken by the French) came here on parole. They give a strange account of French sailors, who are under little or no subordination, and when a breeze of wind comes, would sooner let their sails blow to pieces, than mount their yards to take them in. I am surpris'd how the devil they got here, and this must have been the reason why most of the French lost their masts in the late storm whilst our ships remain'd unhurt. The gentlemen say that the Count treated them whilst on board with genuine politesse and at their departure desir'd, if they were ill treated, or did not like the town they were sent to, they would inform him, and that he would take care they were treated with the respect due British officers, and as for the town, he would order them to any they would nominate.

SEPT: 9TH. The person who brought the Navy officers is the Commissary genl of prisoners. He informs us that several prisoners will be soon exchang'd and that we are to be amongst them; at the same time he gave us an order to go to Rutland where the prisoners are collecting.

SEPT: 10TH. The principal officers are lodg'd in the same house I am. They are Capt: Ingles (who was taken in a sloop of war, looking out for Adml Byron with despatches, and mistook the French for him); Capt: Gambier[1] nephew to the Admiral of the same name—was taken in a bomb vessel, sail'd from New York with Ld Howe; Lt Wentworth, commander of an arm'd ship and—not knowing the French were on the coast—came to an anchor off Sandy Hook in the night with five prizes he had captured—in the morn found himself in the

[1] James first Baron Gambier, naval administrator and Admiral of the Fleet; his uncle, also James Gambier, was second in command under Lord Howe.

[ 38 ]

midst of the French Fleet. These are all the commanders—the others are the complements belonging to their ships.

SEPT: 12TH. Having receiv'd a certificate that we had discharg'd our debts—from one of the Committee—and taken leave of our friends, Brown and me went off in a one horse chair, bag and baggage for Rutland. Got this even to Worcester —a pretty inland town. Went to the gaol to visit an officer of the 62nd Regt—a Mr B——l, put in for breaking his parole. He was confin'd to the same room with a friend of Government—told us he was perfectly happy in his situation and did not seem to desire an enlargement. I believe the man is mad.

SEPT: 13TH. Arriv'd at Rutland. Part of the Convention army being remov'd here for the conveniency of fresh provision we met many friends—and amongst them the officers of our Grenadiers and Light Infantry—with whom we din'd. Capt: Wiseman insists on our making his house our home during our stay.

SEPT: 14TH. Went to a barn to see the remainder of the men taken with us, who, after they had almost been starv'd on board the Guard-ship for eight months, were allow'd to come to this place, where they have a large barn, are allow'd provision and are under no restraint but go where they please. They are reduced to about 50 men including sergeants and corporals. The others have either made their escape, or are working in the country, at places we can send for them. They are shockingly off—in point of clothing; and I am afraid we shall not be able to procure them any, as it seems they are not to be exchang'd with us—Yankee policy to make the men desert.

SEPT: 15TH. A horse race this morn—the loser was to give a rump and dozen. Being one of the guests, just as we had all collected and dinner was serving, I was seiz'd with a vomiting and great head ache; upon this I lay down, but continuing ill, I return'd home with great difficulty. The doctor imagines it a Coup de Soleil.

SEPT: 16TH. My head is still much affected but the sickness is gone.

SEPT: 17TH. So much recover'd as to dine out. Lt Valancy, 62nd Regt, aide de camp to Genl Phillips[1], came from Cambridge and brought an order for us to leave a subaltern officer with the men. There are three of us—we must draw for it— whoever is the unfortunate will be ready to hang himself.

SEPT: 18TH. Was pretty well, but being engag'd to dine out —had scarcely proceeded $\frac{1}{2}$ a mile—when on a sudden turn of my head was taken with such an intense pain over my eyes and grew so giddy that I fell down almost senseless. Capt: Baird who was with me took me up and convey'd me to an house; where being bled I recover'd so far, that with the assistance of two men I got to my inn—but such torment as I felt, I would not wish to my greatest enemy. The least inclination of my head either to the right, or left, made me scream with anguish; it was as if burning iron was run through my brain.

SEPT: 19TH. Every thing tried for my relief. The doctor has rub'd my temples till they are sore. I have snuff'd up strong waters till I have excoriated the inside of my nose—but all in vain. The doctor now says that nothing but patience will get the better of my disorder.

SEPT: 20TH. Wiseman has insisted on my going to his room and taking his bed, as he says I shall be much quieter there.

[1] General William Philips, in command of a brigade of infantry and of the artillery in Burgoyne's force, captured at Saratoga.

He would not allow me to say anything against it. This is an obligation that, I fear, will never be in my power to repay.

Sept: 21st. The doctor has at last found me some relief—by prescribing bark. My head is not subject to those acute pangs that troubled me at first, but has now settled to a severe head ache. Wiseman mixes, and gives me the medicines—himself.

Sept: 25th. From a constant taking of bark, I am now able to sit up and the pains are going off. Threw the dice to see who was to remain behind with the men. Brown was the unfortunate hero but am in hopes he will go with us, as there is an Ensign Rynd of our Regt, who belongs to the Convention; it is thought that upon proper application Genl Phillips will appoint him to the charge of the men.

Sept: 26th. The day after tomorrow is appointed for our departure. I am recovering very fast and make no doubt shall be perfectly well by that time. The only disagreeable consequence attending this sickness is the loss of my hair, which comes out by hand-fulls. I hope it will not all fall out—what a horrid old-fashioned figure shall I make in a wig. I shall be taken for the resurrection of one of Queen Anne's soldiers.

Sept: 27th. Every thing is settled and we have sign'd a parole that, though we go into our lines, we are not to act, or quit the Continent, without being exchang'd, and that if again call'd on we are to return. These are the principal articles.

Sept: 28th. Brown has leave to go with us—Rynd being appointed to take care of our men. After parting with our friends, we march'd off altogether. We make a good show, there being 20 German officers, ten British, and 150 Highlanders of the 71st Regt, who were taken 2 years ago by going into Boston Harbour (thinking it in our possession) after the evacuation. As we have 60 miles to go before we embark—which is to be at a place near Providence—6 of us hired a Jersey waggon for which we pay a guinea pr head. Our company is Captains Davies and Lord of our Regt; Chevalier d'Enterroches ensign of the 62nd Regt; Count Randsau a young German officer; an American girl who chooses to go with him, whom he calls Patty—and myself. As we began our journey late in the day, the roads bad—and our carriage though easy none of the most expeditious—it was ten at night before we reach't Worcester, 14 mile from Rutland. At our arrival every place was taken up. Brown and myself, after knocking up half the people in the town, were just thinking of sleeping in the waggon—when we met Peter Frazer, an Highland officer. He immediately took us to a Mrs Chandlers, a genteel woman who gave two excellent beds.

SEPT: 29TH. Mrs Chandlers insisting on our breakfasting with her, we did so and were introduced to Miss Chandlers, a daughter of hers, a very handsome agreeable young lady. Having taken leave of this hospitable family (with an injunction from the mother that if we ever met with her son, who it seems is in our army, we should let him know they were well), we collected our waggon party and left the town. After an agreeable day's jaunt, we arriv'd at night at Mendon where we had poor food and wretched accommodations, being all obliged to lie in one room (the lady not excepted) in beds that by their dirtiness appear'd to have been clean'd once a year, and they stunk so intolerable that it kept us awake half the night.

SEPT: 30TH. Went off very early from this vile hovel and got to a good inn to breakfast—where we recruited ourselves, and made up for the poor fare of last night. About 2 o'clock we found ourselves within two mile of Providence. Here we halted and being not permitted to enter that town turn'd off the road to a small village call'd Pawtucket. In the middle of this place is a pretty fall of water and several iron mills which gives a romantic appearance to the whole. Tolerable accommodations but much crowded.

OCTOBER 1ST. Capt: Davies gave up his seat to a German officer's lady, she being fatigued with riding. We were all very happy, and our German lady serenaded us with her songs, which were much admir'd—but not understood. By mistaking our road we found ourselves in the midst of Providence before we knew it—however we were soon out again. Near the town (which is large) we saw a large encampment of militia and on the heights they have rais'd some forts—the reason of their having these is their vicinity to Rhode Island, from whence they are often threaten'd with a visit. At night arriv'd at Warwick Neck, the place of embarkation. We had scarcely got to the inn when a guard of blacks and blackguards came to the house with orders not to let us out. Upon our remonstrating against this insult to the Commanding Officer, he told us it was in order to prevent our reconnoitring his camp and give an information at Rhode Island. He is an illiterate fellow, and wants to appear the man of consequence. It seems he has not above 40 men and they are encamped in an orchard—a pretty camp truly.

OCT: 2ND. Obliged to remain—the vessels not being arriv'd to take us off. We cannot prevail on this man to take off his guard, though we show'd him our parole and told him our confinement made it void. The only favour (if it may be call'd so) that he will grant is to extend our limits, and we have now about 200 yards to walk. Davies of ours got into such a passion with this fellow that he wanted to fight him with pistols but the American declin'd it. We were surpris'd about one o'clock at receiving an order from one of the rebel generals to return to Providence, but before we had time to comply, an express came to inform us the first was wrote by mistake— I would we were fairly off.

Oct: 3rd. Sloops being arrived, after paying eighty dollars for the hire of one, most of the officers and servants embarked. We had some difficulty in getting out of the small creek that runs up to Warwick Neck, but when clear we had an agreeable passage sailing between several small islands, one of which was a rebel post where they had cannon. About 10 o'clock at night (being within one mile of Rhode Island) we were brought to by the Sphinx, man of war—one of our guardships. Some of us immediately went on board requesting leave to land, being so much crowded that scarcely half could remain below deck. The captain said it was contrary to orders to allow any person to land after gun-firing and added that, supposing he permitted us, the shore was so entirely guarded by Germans, who would stop us, that t'would be vain to attempt it. Our situation being again urged to him, he sent us his longboat, in which 20 of us immediately push'd off. On our arrival to the shore, the Germans oblig'd us to remain two hours in the boat till such time as they had sent to their camp to know what was to be done with us. At last a German officer arriv'd, who on being informed of our situation permitted us to land, and conducted us to a farm house where we had such fare as they could give us, and a Commissary that was there gave us a cag of rum. Having satisfied our appetites, the next thing was where to lie. There was but three beds in the house— quite insufficient for our numbers. I was preparing some straw for myself in a corner (being the only officer of our Regt there) when the German officers came and insisted I should take part of a bed. I was tired and therefore easily persuaded to accept the offer. Had a German captain for my bed-fellow, who in order (as I suppose) to amuse me, talk'd a good deal in a language neither German or English. Having through politeness attended to him for some time—without understanding even the subject of his discourse—sleep got the better of good manners. How long he talk'd I know not—but suppose till he finish'd his story.

OCT: 4TH. On coming down stairs this morning found all our officers, they having landed about 3 o'clock in the morn. After finishing some bread and milk provided for our breakfast, all marched for Newport, about 8 miles from the place we lay. Pass'd by two encampments, the one British, and the other German, and arriv'd about two o'clock at Newport. Waited on the Commanding Officer, Genl Prescott, who receiv'd us very politely and ordered us quarters. In the evening an officer waited on us with cards from the Genl requesting our company the next day to dinner.

OCT: 5TH. Dined with Genl Prescott. Upon being inform'd my name was Hughes and that I had a brother in his Regt, he was so obliging as to tell me if there was any thing in his power to do for me—upon an application—I might depend on its being perform'd. At our departure he made us a present of a sheep each, as he said fresh provision was very scarce, and there was seldom any sold in the market.

OCT: 6TH. Newport may be reckon'd amongst the largest American towns even now—though near 600 houses have been already destroy'd, either for fuel, or the brick for building barracks (most of these destroy'd houses belonged to the disaffected). Their principal street is above a mile in length and so straight that you see from one end to the other. The harbour, which was one of the most commodious in America, is now almost spoilt by the number of ships sunk to keep the French Fleet from the town, and the wharfs are destroy'd to make platforms for the guns. There are three batteries for the defence of the harbour mounting about 30 pieces of cannon, 24 and 32 pounders—it was these which gave Count d'Estaing such a disagreeable reception. The town itself is not fortified, but within about a mile of it are two lines running across the Island; that nearest the town is form'd of small redoubts connected by a breast work—this is of no great strength—the second line is cannon-proof, has a number of detached forts all along its front and is defended by a stout abattis. Against this the Americans made their grand effort. Their advance batteries was scarcely within 500 yards of a mortar battery in front of the lines—their works though now fill'd up are still visible and were carried on with great regularity. The country within a mile of the works has the most desolate appearance that possibly can be imagin'd. The houses are all burnt for fear they should afford shelter to the enemy, their fences are destroy'd, and their orchards cut to the stumps either for opening the country or making the abattis. In short this island, formerly the Garden of America, is now the picture of war and rapine. The force on this place is about 6000 effective men who are dispers'd in different encampments all over the Island. The troops kept for the defence of the town and lines are two Regt of Germans, one of provincials and one British.

Ocт: 8тн. It being impossible to live under half a guinea pr day at the taverns, Davies, Brown and myself have agreed to mess together and to content ourselves with our rations, and what little we can pick up in the market—which will be nothing but fish. Genl Prescott has inform'd us that we shall go to New York with the first convoy—until our arrival at York we cannot be exchang'd.

OCT: 10TH. Having few or no acquaintance in this town, our time is generally employ'd in walking. Indeed the situation of this town makes our rambles extremely agreeable, as we can always vary them and have generally an extensive prospect. I was today on the south side the town, up at the Signal House. The ground here is very strong and it is thought that if our troops had been oblig'd to have given up the town, they would have retired to these heights from whence they could not easily be dislodg'd. There are two small forts erected on the most commanding spots—one mounting three and the other four pieces of cannon. It is likewise on this piece of ground that the South Battery (which entirely commands the mouth of the harbour) stands, of 6 24 pounders. Sergt Brownhill, who made his escape out of the Guard-ship, came to me. He is appointed to do duty in the 37th Regt.

OCT: 20th. The wood fleet from Long Island arriv'd this morning. At their departure, which will be as soon as possible, we take the benefit of their convoy for our voyage to New York.

OCT: 29TH. Ensn Savory of the 20th Regt arriv'd here with the clothing of the Convention army from Canada. By him received a letter and a few necessaries from my Father—by my letter I am inform'd that Capt: Scott and Ensn Knox of our Regt are both drown'd.

OCT: 30TH. Heard today that the Convention army are to be removed to Virginia. The Yankees pretend they cannot subsist them in New England—for which reason they give them a march of 600 mile which will take them most of the winter.

NOVEMBER 7TH. Six months subsistence being due us, waited on Genl Prescott to desire an order for it. He inform'd us it was out of his power to grant one as we did not belong to his command. He took me aside and said if I wanted cash he would give it me and charge my brother with it. Did not accept the offer—as our officers intend drawing a bill on the agent. However return'd my acknowledgement to the old gentleman for his politesse and attention.

NOV. 10TH. Was agreeably surpris'd at meeting with Ld Balcarres in the street this morning. He is just arriv'd from New York where he has been on parole and is now on his return to the Convention army; but as they have already march'd for Virginia, he intends returning to York and joining them as they cross Hudson River.

NOV. 11TH. The Cornwall, a 74 gun ship of Admiral Byron's squadron, came in here this evening. She says the Fleet met a violent storm in Boston Bay (where they were blocking up the French) in which the Cornwall sprung her main mast, and was obliged to bear away for this port.

NOV: 12TH. A fleet of large vessels appearing off this morn, the batteries were mann'd, as it was not known what they were and they steer'd for the Island. About eleven o'clock our doubts were clear'd by the entrance of Admiral Byron, with one 90 and ten 74 gun ships. Several vessels are missing —and most of the ships receiv'd damage in the late gale of wind.

NOV: 14TH. The Somerset, a 64 gun ship of Admiral Byron's squadron, has been wreck'd on Cape Cod—most of the men escaped but are made prisoners. Count d'Estaing has taken this opportunity of sailing from Boston—it is imagin'd for the West Indies, where they may do great mischief as our force there is not capable of opposing them. Adml Byron's stay will be longer than was at first expected, as the Fleet must water.

Nov: 16th. Savory being appointed an assistant engineer, went to see him at work. They are strengthening the outer line with a four-bastioned square fort—almost complete, and mounts 12 pieces of cannon on the curtains. On my return met Capt: Welsh, Genl Prescott's aide de camp, who inform'd me I should sail for York in a few days.

Nov: 17th. The captain of the Sultan—a 74 gun ship— having died, he was buried this morning with the honours of war. The corpse was brought on shore attended by all the boats of the Fleet—the rowers all dress'd in white shirts and black caps. The instant the body was put into the boat the Sultan fir'd minute guns and continued them till the whole was over. A German Regt was drawn up at the landing, who conducted the body to the church and after the interment fired three volleys. The whole was performed with solemnity and regularity and was so affecting that I observ'd most of the ladies shed tears.

Have had great difficulty in procuring cash for bills, the merchants being extremely cautious, as within these six months there has been protests to the amount of thirty thousand pounds. Ld Balcarres very obligingly endors'd ours, which has remov'd all scruples. Receiv'd orders to embark to-morrow for York.

Nov: 18th. Embark'd in a large transport, but the wind not being favourable return'd on shore to dine—lay on board at night. In the ship are six officers, 53rd Regt—Lieut Bliss (son of Mrs Bliss with whom I lived at Concord), two Highland officers who came with us from Rutland and all their men (about 200). We carry eight guns.

Nov: 19TH. Sail'd from Newport, but had scarcely proceeded two leagues when the wind chang'd and we were obliged to put back.

Nov: 20TH. Took our final departure from Rhode Island. Our fleet consists of near forty sail—mostly small vessels. Our convoy consists of the Sphinx, sloop of war (who is only to see us beyond New London and return), the Halifax, arm'd brig mounting 16 guns and two or three small tenders of 10 or 12 guns each. The wind fair till we doubled Point Judith, when it blew right in our teeth—tack'd on and off all night.

Nov: 21ST. Foul wind—gain'd about 8 leagues during the day. At night anchored close under an island for fear any of us might be pick'd up by some lurking privateer.

Nov: 22ND. We got today into the Sound; the wind as yesterday—make but little way. At night anchored 5 leagues to the eastward of New London.

Nov: 23RD. Past New London but at such a distance we could only observe the light house at the mouth of the harbour —the wind unfavourable.

Nov: 24TH. The Sphinx, having perform'd her charge, left us.

Nov: 25TH. Entertain'd with a chase between one of our tenders, and a rebel sloop—the tender fired several shot, but the sloop escap'd. Past New Haven. The view of the Connecticut shore is extremely pleasant, being well cultivated and thickly inhabited. On an eminence about a mile up the country observ'd a fort and encampment. Had a brisk gale— and a short rocking sea—which spoilt my appetite.

## November 1778

Nov: 26TH. The wood fleet and convoy left us—they went into Huntingdon Bay, Long Island. A fair wind carried us pleasantly up the Sound, which is so narrow at Whitestone, where we anchor'd in the even, that a musket might be fired across. About a league from hence passed the Raven, guardship. This is the place Ld Howe cross'd his army, just before the engagement of White Plains;[1] the continental side is call'd Frog Neck.

Nov: 27TH. The wind contrary—weigh'd anchor at ebb which pusht us a little forward. Went on shore and procur'd some eatables.

Nov: 28TH. Our captain intends tiding it down; just as we had rais'd our anchor—our ship stuck fast on a mud bank. After several fruitless attempts to get her off, we were oblig'd to let her remain. The next flood will float her.

Nov: 29TH. The two last ebbs carried us about 3 leagues forward; we can proceed no farther without a pilot, the navigation being very dangerous.

Nov: 30TH. Being very tired of this slow mode of sailing, and a boat offering to carry us to New York in 3 hours, we accepted it; had enchanting views on each side—pass'd through Hell's Gate, but it being almost low water did not see it to

---

[1] After the loss of Boston (see note on p. 21) it was decided to make New York the British base. Sir William Howe's assault upon it opened with the seizure of Staten Island (July 1776). Thence troops were landed on Long Island where, near Brooklyn, Washington's main defences were placed. The approaches to these were captured at the engagement of Flat Bush (see p. 56) but Washington was able to withdraw his whole force to New York Island itself. Howe attempted a flanking movement to the eastward through Long Island Sound; but Washington, retiring up the New York peninsula, established a strong position at White Plains before Howe was ready to join battle. Howe did not take decisive action and the American army disengaged to the northward.

perfection. This is the most difficult place for a ship to pass of any in the Sound—it is not above 500 yards across and the tide rushes through with such velocity that it occasions a number of eddies and whirlpools; one of which, call'd the Pot, boils and roars even in calm weather as if it was agitated by a hurricane. If any vessel gets into this Pot—she is twirl'd round several times and then cast on shore; a frigate was serv'd thus a few days since. Just at the entrance of this pass the rebels rais'd a fort to prevent our ships passing up the Sound— before we had possession of York Island. The tide failing, we landed four miles from the town, and walk'd in. About 12 o'clock we got to Hick's Tavern and ordered breakfast, but the good lady of the mansion not liking our garb told us it would be dinner-time soon and that she would not be troubled with boiling the tea kettle. One of our servants entering just then, and informing them who we were, every person became amazingly obsequious. Gave us breakfast and at five a good dinner. In the evening went to the Coffee House—in return- ing from whence by the attraction of musick was led to a large house before which were 20 or 30 musicians—all martial; it had so good an effect that I did not observe one sad face amongst the numerous group that were collected by the occasion. It being difficult to get lodging, by way of great favour—Governor Franklin being out of town—had his apartments for this night.

Nov: 31st. Capt: Baird waited on Sir Henry Clinton who ordered us quarters. On calling for our bill had a guinea each to pay—a moderate sum for one day. As we thought ourselves imposed upon, went to Smith's Tavern who only charges 7 shillings pr head for dinner—Hick's charg'd 12. After dinner was call'd out by a gentleman—whom to my great surprise I found to be Griff Ridsdale. Griff took me to his lodgings which he begs me to use as my own and desires I will always breakfast with him. By him, am inform'd that my brother is at Jamaica, Long Island with the Grenadiers— 12 miles from hence.

DECEMBER 1ST. Cross'd the ferry to Brooklyn, Long Island. Ridsdale went with me and try'd several places to procure me a horse, but not being able to succeed, I walk'd to Jamaica where I found to my mortification that the Grenadier Company of the 7th Regt, to which my brother belong'd, had march'd two or three days before on a detachment to New Utrecht—16 miles from Jamaica. Being too much fatigued (from having perform'd the first walk in boots) to undertake a second of such length, I was musing what course to pursue —just then observ'd a man of the 33rd; on asking who commanded their company found it to be my friend Oakes— immediately went to his house, found him there and remain'd with him all night.

DEC: 2ND. Parted with Oakes who lent me his horse to go to Utrecht, where I found William after a separation of 7 years; the alteration was so great that he hardly knew me. From my brother learnt that all the family were well and wanted to have me home. Will desires that I will live with him and Capt: Hume—with this, as it entirely corresponds with my own desires, I shall readily comply.

DEC: 4TH. About 8 o'clock in the morn an express arriv'd to Capt: Hume to march with the troops here directly for Brooklyn. About 9 we all march'd, and in one hour and a half reacht the ferry—distant 8 miles. Here they were join'd by all the Grenadiers and Light Infantry, who are to be reinforc'd by other troops and are to be sent up the North

River, suppos'd for the intent of liberating some of the Convention army who are now crossing it. Left my brother and cross'd the ferry to New York with an intention of seeing him as he passed through. Having finish'd some little business went to the wharf where the troops embark'd—found my brother already on board and the ship under way—shall be anxious for their return. Met the officers of our Regt.

New York is situated at the confluence of two rivers, the one call'd the North or Hudson, the other the East; this is not so properly a river as an arm of the sea, it being the channel which separates Long Island from the continent and forms the Sound. Hudson River runs up the country past Albany—to which town small country vessels run up, being 150 mile, and men of war may sail 100 mile up—having a bold shore, good depth of water and a channel from $\frac{1}{2}$ a mile to 2 mile wide. The town formerly extended on both of these, but since the commencement of the present rebellion most part of the city lying on the North River has been maliciously burnt by incendiaries employ'd by the Americans—for the sake of distressing us, and ruining those who show an attachment to our cause by remaining under our protection. On the East River (which forms a safe and capacious harbour) the town is chiefly built and runs about 1 mile and $\frac{1}{2}$. Here the water is so deep that 74 gun ships may lay their sides to the wharfs. At the upper end of this range are the King's Yards for repairing ships and building boats. There is no dock, nor have they materials for building men of war; the principal work is the making of masts for ships of the line, which is of great service —formerly large ships dismasted were obliged to return home for new ones.

The town may contain four thousand houses, mostly stone

or brick, and was formerly embellisht with many publick works but these have felt the effects of civil violence, in particular two statues, one of George and the other of Chatham both so mutilated that without information none could imagine what they were intended for. They have a Town House, Merchants' Hall, two large hospitals, a gaol, and a vast number of churches —the principal of which, St Paul's, has escap'd the fire though the houses round it are burnt to their foundations. The markets are plentifully supplied with all sorts of meat and vegetables from Long Island but are at present immoderately dear. Good fish is scarce but they have oysters by shiploads. New York has no regular fortifications nor do I think it capable of any. Its defence towards the water is a battery of 40 or 50 pieces of cannon, erected at the point of land where the rivers join, and commands both—though not sufficiently to prevent ships passing, which an enemy might do with little injury either from this battery or from the fort of Paulus Hook on the Jersey side of the water; but as New York stands 30 miles from the sea and there are several passages commanded by different forts, ships must run the ⟨? gauntlet⟩ through the fire of these, not to mention a respectable naval force always in the harbour. Towards the land 4 or 5 small detach'd forts are all its strength; but here as by water the access is the difficult point, the passes of King's Bridge—and Haarlem—which are strongly fortified prevent any hostile approach. The force at present at New York and its dependencies—Long Island, Staten Island &c—under Sir H. Clinton is about 20,000 men, British, German and provincial.

DEC: 6TH. 50 of Burgoyne's men who had made their escape arriv'd here today. The guide who conducted them was allow'd 1 guinea pr man.

[ 55 ]

DEC: 9TH. Was surpris'd this morning at my brother's coming into my room before I was up. The troops are return'd from the expedition up the North River, after having proceeded as high as King's Ferry, but the Conventioners had all cross'd two days before. Went with my brother to Utrecht.

DEC: 11TH. Our amusement here is that of duck shooting. The ducks are so numerous that without exaggeration I am certain I have seen above a thousand of a morn. The best time for shooting them is when the wind obliges them to keep close in shore—in fair weather they are always at a great distance and they are too shy to approach them with boats. The people make use of a decoy in winter, by painting their boats white, hiding themselves and then floating like a lump of ice. By this finesse they will get amongst flocks and kill 30 of a shot.

DEC: 13TH. The 16th Dragoons embark'd for England under convoy of the Bedford, a 74 gun ship of Admiral Byron's, who is gone with the remainder of the Fleet to the West Indies where Count d'Estaing now is.

DEC: 19TH. The rebels having cross'd in boats by night and plunder'd the inhabitants, Capt: Murry's troop of Light Horse were sent here to patrol the coast.

DEC: 22ND. Went to York and having some leisure view'd the ground the rebels retir'd to after their defeat at Flat Bush.[1] It is a heighth above Brooklyn which they had fortified with several small forts connected by a breast work and cover'd by an abattis—the breast work and abattis are now destroy'd but most of the forts are still preserv'd, one in particular built round a hill in the shape of a cork screw. Most of the officers blame Sir Wm Howe for not storming these works immediately after the engagement, as the rebels were panick-struck

[1] See note on p. 51.

and our pursuit so close that we must have enter'd with the fugitives; the consequence of which would have been the rebel army surrendering to the amount of 15,000 men or, if they would not surrender, they might have been pusht into the East River, which prevented a retreat. This would have ended the rebellion at once, but who could be so cruel as to sacrifice such a number of poor men?—besides it would have hinder'd the commander making his fortune. O tempora! O mores!

DEC: 23RD. Again at New Utrecht; very severe weather —and a snow storm.

DEC: 24TH. Frost bit both my hands—by taking a duck that I had shot out of the water. Have attempted to recover them by snow but with little success as they are still extremely painful.

DEC: 26TH. There are a number of rebel officers on parole near here, and to show what a set of beings some of them are, shall relate a small incident that occur'd today. A stranger came to Capt: Hume and lodg'd a complaint against a man whom he had heard speak disrespectfully of the King. The person inform'd against was sent for; in a little time a droll diminutive figure (in a blue coat faced red, a brown waist-coat patch'd with all the colours of the rainbow and a greasy pair of leather breeches) presented himself as the culprit. He was very impertinent and answered interrogatories with a contemptuous sneer. At last it was demanded who he was—I have the honour of serving as Lieutenant in the American service and am at present a prisoner on parole. Pray Sir what was your business at such a house? I was mending a pr of breeches for the landlord. Enough Sir; be pleas'd to return to your work but be more guarded in your discourse—and the tailor with a low scrape (to show his breeding) retired.

DEC: 28TH. A servant whom I had left in York came here and with a most doleful lamentable phiz and voice inform'd me the rebels had demanded us and that the 2nd of next month was fixed for our being deliver'd to their Commissary at Elizabethtown. This intelligence surprises me, as we have been always told we should never be sent back but be kept in lieu of several of their officers who had violated their paroles. To be provided against the worst, I have got all the tailors in the neighbourhood to make me clothes.

## January 1779

JANUARY 1ST. Went to New York with a heavy heart and found all my brothers in adversity as sorrowful as myself. We are respited for two days and are not to depart till the 4th. This is something like men to be hang'd whose execution is put off —and we are now in hopes we shall not go at all. Indeed I think we are too sanguine.

JAN: 2ND. Memorial'd Sir Henry Clinton requesting (as we were to return to the enemy) that he would grant us some pay. Two months are order'd us which is not sufficient to clear my debts in this town so that, had not my brother been here, I should have return'd destitute of clothes and not a farthing in my pocket. This is the more inexcusable as we have four months due. If our friends treat us in this manner —what may we expect from our enemies?

JAN: 3RD. Met Col: York at the Coffee House. On hearing of my recall, he gave me the names of some families at Philadelphia to call on in his name, and he said they would do anything to serve me. Am now ready to depart at a moment's warning. Tomorrow 8 o'clock is the time fix'd.

JAN: 4TH. At 11 o'clock sail'd from New York, at two landed at our advance post on Staten Island where we are oblig'd to remain, as the ice floats in such large shoals that no vessel can venture amongst it. This post is a stone house fortified with loop-holes and an abattis—it is garrison'd by a part of the 26th Regt. The officers have divided us amongst them and we are in their apartments. The unfortunate fellows accompanying us are 17 German officers, two of the 71st, and three Conventioners—Capt: Strangeways, 24th, Cambell and England, 62nd.

# The Journal of Thomas Hughes

Jan: 6th. The ice being mostly gone, sail'd to the point two miles from Elizabethtown where we landed. A rebel guard posted here took charge of us till the arrival of one Col: Beatie, the rebel Commissary, to whom we were delivered—like so many sheep to the slaughter—by Mr Loring. Two officers of the 71st and the three Conventioners were permitted to return to New York, but we ill-fated youths went with the Germans to Elizabethtown where we were civilly treated and had a good tavern.

Jan: 7th. Elizabethtown is a large straggling place in New Jersey and may contain 700 houses. It is at present the advance post of Washington's army where he has about 800 men station'd, under the command of a Genl Maxwell, formerly a school master, the most ungentlelike looking fellow I ever saw—and by accounts his appearance does not belie him. I am surpris'd our people allow them to remain here unmolested, this being but 14 miles from York, and Washington's army by which (if attack'd) they must be supported lies above 20 miles inland. Three men, who call'd themselves Justices, came to our tavern and ordered us to appear before them. On our compliance they made us produce our paper money which did not exceed 150 dollars; on inspection they pronounc'd it counterfeit—took it away—and would not let us have the satisfaction of seeing it destroyed, though we desired it.

Jan: 8th. Saw Genl Lee[1] this morn. He is a short little man with an aquiline nose and has not the least appearance of a soldier. Lee is a striking example of the unsettled tottering situation of those who build upon public favour. At the commencement of this war, he was their idol—nothing could

[1] See note 1 on p. 33.

be well done without Genl Lee. Now what a change! mention his name and it's curst and execrated—traitor, coward, villain, are his most gentle epithets—and all this because he did not beat at Monmouth the flower of the British Army, with 8000 ill-disciplin'd, ill-arm'd Americans. He is not now recovered of a wound receiv'd in a duel fought about a month ago. At the time of his fighting he had 7 challenges from officers in his pocket—to whom he had given no other offence, than saying he did not think they could stand against British Grenadiers.

JAN: 9TH. A dirty wet disagreeable day. At two o'clock we were sent off in waggons towards Easton where we are to remain on parole. About ten at night arriv'd at a small town and were quartered off at the different houses—Capt: Lord and me got into the house of a civil genteel family.

JAN: 10TH. Breakfasted at the Scotch Plains—pass'd through the gap in the mountains where we had some of the most romantick scenes imaginable and at night lay at Stony-ridge within 3 miles of Washington's camp.

JAN: 11TH. Breakfasted at Pluckemin where all the rebel artillery is station'd. At night were quarter'd off in private houses; at the house I was the people gave us a liquor distill'd from peaches—a fiery disagreeable spirit.

JAN: 12TH. Ante Mer:—Our landlady by way of great favour offered to kill us a goose for breakfast; but we are obliged to go off without eating—having a dangerous river to pass.

Post Mer:—We were 5 hours crossing a small river which had overflowed its banks and was froze hard enough to bear men; but our waggons plung'd through—and one overset directly in the middle which occasion'd much difficulty before

[ 61 ]

it was got up again. This night lay at little Germantown—a place of small note, but pleasantly situated.

JAN: 13TH. Reach'd Pittstown—which is small and lies in a vale; lodg'd at a doctor's, a friend to Government. He had two or three pretty daughters and we spent the time very agreeable.

JAN: 14TH. Our road this day lay over the mountains and as our carriage is none of the most expeditious—it was very tiresome. At night lay at a small town (where were some iron mines) within 7 miles of Easton.

JAN: 15TH. Cross'd the Delaware to Easton; the river is about 500 yards wide and very rapid. As the town is small and a Regt of soldiers are quartered in it we had difficulty in procuring lodgings. At last got wretchedly accommodated at a one floor inn—my room is ankle deep in water.

JAN: 16TH. Our present Commissary—Col: Hooper—has behaved with the greatest civility. Instead of confining us (as others in his employment used to do) to two or three miles, he has given us the whole county of Northampton. His only request was that we should not sleep out of the town without first acquainting him.

Easton is a small but regular town all the streets intersecting at right angles. The houses are mostly of one floor and the inhabitants Dutch or German emigrants.[1] They have a church and Town House—the latter is spoilt by being made a barrack for troops. The town lies in a small plain with the Delaware in front, the Lehigh, a large river, on one side—and the Bush-kill (a rivulet full of trout) on the other; both these fall into

[1] New York was in origin a Dutch colony and German emigrants had settled there and in Pennsylvania in considerable numbers in the eighteenth century.

the Delaware within half a mile of the town and are boundaries to the small plain on which it stands. The view from hence is very contracted as we are surrounded with hills; the most extensive one is just across the Delaware to the Jersey shore where there is a small village. We are now in the province of Pennsylvania—the mildest and most fruitful of the thirteen States.

JAN: 18TH. The Delaware being partly frozen—went and skated on it. Found some soldiers fishing, which is perform'd by cutting a hole through the ice and dropping a hook and line through—indeed it is but poor sport and nothing but the fear of starving would make me undertake it. I observ'd several ragged fellows sitting and shivering and if they caught one in half an hour thought themselves well rewarded.

JAN: 28TH. Not being able to procure private lodging, we have agreed to live entirely at a tavern. Our most disagreeable attendant is the noise of the American soldiers who vociferate their songs so loud that the whole house rings with War and Washington, a favourite ballad. In every other respect the men behave very well and even treat us with more civility than their own officers.

FEBRUARY. A dull month—the trees in bloom and a severe frost which kill'd all the fruit.

MARCH. The Indians having committed great havock in the back-settlements, the Regt station'd here march'd to reinforce the fort at Wyoming. Their men appear'd very averse to fight against Indians and many swore they would desert the first opportunity. The whole Regt mustered less than 200—and this is the two Regts drafted into one. Still remain in taverns—every day receive news of an exchange and the day after proves the former a lie. As I believe none, am never deceiv'd. A man call'd Hughes—a Col: in the American service—who lives in the neighbourhood, pretends to be a relation of mine and wants me to come and see him. I suppose some rebel rascal who wants to appear a gentleman —refused.

APRIL. All my amusement at present is trout-fishing which, as they are in great plenty, is very entertaining. The inhabitants have a droll way of catching the shad, a fish I never saw in England. Its make is like the herring but much larger —weighing from three to eight pound. The spring is the only time for catching them as they are then fat and run up the rivers in shoals to spawn. The mode of taking them is as follows—all the inhabitants of a district assemble and go to some part of the river where it's shallow; they all enter the river and being distributed across it begin their first piece of work which is building a dam of loose stones forming an angle, the bottom of which is left open and a net placed to receive the fish. This finish'd, they go 5 or 6 miles up the river, where they cut a good many branches of fir and tie them together till they reach from one side to the other—this piece of handiwork sails down with the stream and the people follow themselves in canoes beating the water and shouting to drive the fish before them. When they have driven all the shad into the lower net, they stop up the entrance with stones, and then let the waters off by throwing down the dam—they often catch three or four thousand at a sweep. What is not for immediate use, they salt in barrels.

MAY 2ND. An expedition being plann'd against the Indians under the command of Genl Sullivan,[1] two of the Regts to be employ'd arriv'd here. Both scarcely muster 300 men.

[1] Major-General Sullivan, one of Washington's most reliable subordinates.

## May 1779

MAY 4TH. The troops mutinied at even rollcalling and swore they would shoot their officers if their pay was not given them—it seems they have four months due. It was promis'd and that quieted them.

MAY 5TH. Our cash being out sent a memorial to Sir Henry Clinton requesting subsistence.

MAY 6TH. A Sergt and thirty men belonging to the troops here deserted last night, carrying off their arms, ammunition and accoutrements.

MAY 7TH. Genl Sullivan arriv'd and made a speech to the soldiers for two hours—the length of it is not so very extra-ordinary when it is considered the speaker of it was formerly an attorney. Amongst many other promises in this elaborate discourse, he told the men if they had any complaints against their officers—he would redress them. On this, a soldier complain'd of the adjutant—for which as soon as the Genl was gone he was severely beaten.

MAY 9TH. The troops march'd for their rendezvous (which I believe is to be at Wyoming) where it is intended to collect 4 or 5 thousand men and carry the war into the Indian country.

MAY 14TH. Receiv'd an order to go to Lancaster on parole—80 miles from hence. This is a distressing circum-stance as our money is expended and we are considerably in debt to the inn-keeper.

MAY 16TH. Having inform'd Col: Hooper of our situation, he very generously lent us two thousand dollars which will pay our paper debts and carry us to the journey's end.

MAY 18TH. March'd from Easton—they have provided us a waggon if we grow tir'd and choose to ride. Our conductor is a Capt: Keasely, a genteel sort of man, who says he will make ⟨it⟩ as agreeable to us as he can. Only walked 12 miles to the town of Bethlehem—a neat pleasant place on the banks of the Lehigh. The inhabitants are Moravians, a sect who have establish'd rules which every one in the society is obliged to comply with; one is that all their young un-married men live together in one large house and are call'd the Brotherhood, and all their young women in another who are call'd the Sisterhood. In these houses every trade is carried on and they never permit but one of each; by this means their interests never clash and they make a point of never purchasing of another what they can buy from their own people. To this may be ascribed the goodness of their tavern—their having but one—and it is far the best of any we have found out of York.

MAY 19TH. Breakfasted at Allentown. At night lay at a small inn by the road-side. Had but poor accommodations and could procure no liquor but peach-spirit.

MAY 20TH. Being tir'd of walking, we all got into our waggon. In the afternoon our cavalcade entered Reading. On our arrival at the tavern, five officers of the 82nd Regt (on parole here) waited on us and desired our company at supper. These gentlemen were ship-wreckt on the coast—about two months ago; some of them are not yet recover'd of the fatigue sustain'd on that occasion, as the ship foundered and they remain'd 48 hours on the rigging.

MAY 21ST. The want of waggons detaining us, it afforded an opportunity of viewing the town. Reading is a neat regular town on the banks of the Schuylkill. They have a Town House, Market House, gaol and two or three churches. The private houses are well built and altogether it has more the appearance of an English town than any I have seen since my departure from York. The Schuylkill is only navigable here for boats. This place like Easton lies in a plain and is mostly surrounded with hills. About 12 o'clock we forded the river and proceeded on our journey. Put up in the even at Rheems —a paltry dirty little village and not worth mentioning.

MAY 22ND. At Lancaster—where we have an excellent tavern. On our arrival were delivered to a Mr Henry, who has the charge of us in the absence of a Mr Atlee (our Commissary). To Mr Henry we were oblig'd to sign a parole—the limits only one mile—which he says is the positive orders of the Commissary we shall not exceed.

MAY 24TH. Lancaster is the largest inland town in North America, but it makes no appearance till you are got into it as it lies in a bottom. The buildings are good and the whole town being lay'd out in squares (according to Penn's plan) makes it look very regular and pretty. The Court House stands in the centre from whence the principal streets lead in straight lines; they have a Market House, gaol and several churches—one of which is an English one but they have at present no service, as the parson taking the contrary side in the disputes was obliged to fly the country. The town contains about 800 houses and 6000 inhabitants. The country round here is esteem'd the most fertile of any in Pennsylvania for grain. The most material want experienced at Lancaster is that of a river— though that is in some measure remedied by a small creek, which runs within a mile, and turns a number of mills. Lee's Regt[1] of Light Horse are station'd here at present; their barracks are on the verge of the town and are surrounded by a strong stoccade 20 feet high, defended by four bastion log-

[1] Colonel Henry Lee, Washington's best cavalry officer.

houses. This Regt is the best appointed corps of any I have seen in America, they being extremely well mounted, well clothed and all stout young fellows.

MAY 26TH. Mr Atlee, the Commissary, being arrived, waited on him to complain of the smallness of our limits. He says it is not in his power to enlarge them without orders from his superiors but promises to write the Board of War in our favour. I look on this entirely as an excuse—certainly Mr Atlee has as much power here as Col: Hooper had at Easton.

MAY 29TH. Have been looking out these several days for lodgings but cannot procure any—the inhabitants say they are afraid to take in British officers, as they shall be accounted Tories. A blessed state of liberty, where people cannot do what they please with their own houses.

JUNE 4TH. With difficulty have got a lodging. Entirely out of cash and cannot find a person to give us money for a bill. Sent a strong memorial to Sir Henry—if it fails, our only alternative is the gaol.

JUNE 16TH. Lee's Regt of Light Horse march'd for Washington's camp. Sir Henry Clinton is gone up the North River and it is reported the American army are gone after him; if true, it may bring on a general action which will determine the contest.

JUNE 18TH. Received a bill for £150 sterling from New York—this has put us in good humour again as we can pay off some debts due people that want their money.

JUNE 20TH. Walking this morn observ'd 8 or 10 bird as large and very like turkeys; they are called Turkey Buzzards and live on carrion. These are not good to eat—but they have wild turkeys in the woods which will weigh thirty pounds and are esteem'd great dainties.

## June 1779

JUNE 30TH. The Whigs have been greatly elevated of late, by accounts of a defeat of our troops under Genl Prevost[1] in South Carolina—but it proves entirely fiction; instead of a defeat our troops have been victorious in several skirmishes.

JULY 4TH. This day being the anniversary of American Independence, the militia paraded in great pomp and fired; but in the afternoon these sons of liberty being a little elated took it into their heads to attack a set of the chief people in the town who were making merry at a tavern on this joyous occasion. The only reason for this assault was the militia being affronted at the gentlemen drinking by themselves—they thinking that there ought to be no distinction but all get drunk together. The affair ended in breaking some windows—for on this salutation the gentlemen (as they call themselves) sallied out sword in hand and routed the mobile. I am in hopes it will not end so quietly as the vanquish'd denounce vengeance.

JULY 6TH. Genl Thompson—just come out of York on parole—waited on us and was so polite as to offer whatever money we stood in need of. We declin'd the favour. It seems this gentleman has been treated with civility by our officers and particularly so by Sir Guy Carleton—in return for which he says he cannot do less than assist every British officer in distress. This gentleman was taken at Trois-Rivières in Canada on the 9th of June 1776.

JULY 10TH. The mob rose this even—and paraded through the streets to beat the gentleman party. One unfortunate hero fell into their hands and they thrash'd him very handsomely.

JULY 22ND. Genl Clinton having advanc'd up the North

[1] Governor of East Florida, where many Loyalists from the southern colonies had rallied; had collected a force for the raiding of the Carolinas, and was operating from the newly captured base of Savannah.

River and erected two forts, return'd to New York leaving as he imagin'd sufficient garrisons to defend them. The Americans have taken advantage of his absence—attacked and carried the post of Stony Point under the command of Col: Johnson of the 17th Regt; they kill'd or took 500 men. This success as usual has rais'd their spirits and they say it's folly for Britain to attempt a war with America.

JULY 29TH. Genl Sullivan having gone into the Indian country—a party of savages in return have fallen on the frontiers and committed great depredations.

AUGUST 3RD. Col: Johnson and most of the officers taken at Stony Point came here on parole. The wounded were permitted to go to York and their men are sent to Philadelphia gaol—they were all plundered. Their capture seems to have been occasion'd by having too extensive works—and if blame is due the Commanding Officer, it is for attempting to defend his out-works when he had not sufficient troops to man his innermost. By this error the rebels got possession of the strongest defence without opposition and fired from thence on the garrison defending their abattis.

AUGT 12TH. Procur'd leave to go to the Susquehanna River with a party of girls. The ride was 10 miles and the day past very agreeably—cross'd the river which is near 2 miles over, but it has such a number of shallows and falls that it is not navigable even for boats. In the even returned.

AUGT 14TH. Went today on another party of pleasure to see some iron mills—were treated very politely by the proprietor with whom we dined. On our return pass'd through Lititz a small Moravian town; they permitted us to see their church which is small and ornamented with the passions of Our Saviour—not by the most masterly hand.

# *August* 1779

AUGT 18TH. Mr Mersereau, Commissary of Prisoners for New England, pass'd through here in his way to Virginia —for the intent (as he says) to conduct Genl Phillips to New York; but it is strongly imagin'd that the purport of his journey is to bring back his wife, who went off with one of the Conventioners—a Mr Smyth of the Artillery. Alas! poor Joshua—thou art almost as mad as Orpheus; who but a madman would travel 700 mile for a New England wife?

AUGT 22ND. As some officers were sitting at the doors with ladies last night (which is the custom of this country) several rascals flung stones and threatened to beat them if they remain'd out after 9 at night. Mr Atlee has behaved very well on this occasion having oblig'd one of the fellows to give 10,000 dollars bail not to insult us more.

AUGT 29TH. Dr Horn and Mr Horndon—two gentlemen taken at Stony Point but permitted to go into New York—arrived here today. They give intelligence of a reinforcement of troops and ships at New York under Adml Arbuthnot.

SEPTEMBER 4TH. The news of the day is that Spain has declar'd war against Great Britain.[1]

SEPT: 10TH. Went with a party of gentlemen to the Susquehanna. Our landlady at the tavern treated us very uncivilly and at last openly abused us.

SEPT: 19TH. About 100 vagabonds gathered by beat of drum with an intention of insulting the British officers—but our good allies, the gentlemen of the town, went and dispers'd them.

[1] Further French diplomacy had been successful (see note 2 on p. 33). In June 1779 Spain declared war on England.

SEPT: 23RD. Genls Phillips and Reidesel[1] of the Conventioners came here on their way to York to remain there on parole. Their American conductor had a list of other officers who were to go in—my name was amongst them and I am in great hopes of being at York by the end of next month.

SEPT: 28TH. Our people having sent 700 men to establish a post at Penobscot, New Hampshire, the rebels fitted out a large armament to take them. Before they could effect their design Sir George Collier with a few ships fell on their fleet consisting of 40 sail and took or destroy'd the whole. This being an uninhabited part of the coast the army which they had landed will be oblig'd to explore their way back through thick woods—where it's probable most of them will perish. Our troops are station'd at Penobscot to protect the mast cutters—this country being famous for fine timber.

SEPT: 30TH. Seven soldiers broke gaol last night by undermining the wall—being confin'd in the dungeon.

OCTOBER 3RD. All hopes of a speedy exchange are now over—the Commissaries having quarrelled on some trifling subject which may occasion our stay here all winter.

OCT: 5TH. The mob rose at Philadelphia on account of the high price of provision—which are scarcely to be purchas'd for Congress money. Amongst their riots, they attempted to pull down a house, which produced a skirmish between the military and populace. Some people were kill'd and wounded on both sides—the rioters are not yet quell'd.

[1] Baron Riedesel had charge of the German troops in Burgoyne's force and had been captured at Saratoga.

[ 72 ]

OCT: 8TH. A second reinforcement are arrived at York—intelligence that our troops are preparing for some grand expedition.[1] It is high time as the summer has slipt away and nothing worth mentioning yet performed.

OCT: 10TH. Genl Sullivan's expedition against the Indians has met with success—having march'd into their country, beat them in one engagement and destroy'd their settlements. The Indians are not yet so far humbled as to sue for peace.

OCT: 13TH. Saw an opossum with nine young. It is an ugly animal about the size (and not unlike) a pig of two months old. This animal is remarkable for having a false belly—into which the young ones creep (at the approach of danger) and the mother carries them off. They are common in the woods here and it is not unusual for the country people to eat them but they are first obliged to bury them for a day or two—to take off their rank smell.

OCT: 15TH. Count d'Estaing[2] is again on this coast with his squadron and it is given out that the French are to block up the port of New York—whilst Washington with his troops besiege it. The militia are all ordered to be in readiness and magazines of provision and ammunition are collecting in the Jerseys.

OCT: 17TH. Complaints having been lodg'd to the Board of War against us they sent orders for our always being at home by 9 at night. We have positively refus'd compliance—I imagine we shall hear no more of it.

[1] The attempt to consolidate the Loyalists in the southern states by the capture of Charlestown.

[2] D'Estaing, after his failure in the summer of 1778, withdrew to the West Indies and Clinton took the opportunity to capture Savannah and occupy Georgia. D'Estaing returned in September 1779, but, failing again, withdrew to France. This made possible the expedition to Charlestown.

Oct: 20th. The French Fleet are now off Savannah in Georgia which they intend taking before they attack New York. We have 2 or 3000 men entrench'd there under Genl Prevost—who will give good account of both American and French that dare attack him.

Oct: 24th. The Americans are grown heartily tired of this war—even those who a few months ago hated the name of an Englishman now openly court our friendship and tell us they wish a reconciliation could take place; and the country appears as ready now for an alteration of measures as they were when the rebellion commenc'd. This turn of affairs is not owing to any latent friendship for Great Britain—for the rebels in general have not the least spark of gratitude; but it arises entirely from the mismanagement of their rulers, the disaffection of their troops, the depreciation of their paper currency and their immense taxes. These complicated distresses seem to have opened their eyes towards their own safety; and it is the fear of the consequences that may ensue should we succeed that induces them to make their peace. In short they are sensible they deserve hanging and they would fain slip their necks out of the halter. This observation is entirely founded on their behaviour; at the receipt of good news their insolence is insufferable, but bad affects their coward hearts, and they fawn like beaten spaniels.

October. That the Colonies will again be under the jurisdiction of Great Britain, is (in my opinion) a thing of course; my only fear is that, at the time of pacification, the lenity of the mother country will leave the seeds of rebellion still in the country—which perhaps will again blaze forth at a period when it will be impossible to stop it.

Oct: 26th. Genl Hand, one of the commanding officers

against the Indians, is just arriv'd in this town. The troops employ'd on that expedition are on their return to join Genl Washington on the North River having (as 'tis reported) entirely destroy'd the towns of the Five Nations with the inconsiderable loss of 40 men.

OCT: 30TH. The want of cash obliges us to borrow paper money to be paid for in solid coin—we are allow'd 25 paper dollars for one silver but had we ready specie we could get 50. As this reduces us to half pay, wrote to Sir Henry Clinton to complain of our situation and desire pay may be regularly sent us.

NOVEMBER 2ND. Genls Reidesel and Phillips are stop'd at Bethlehem and it is doubtful whether they will be permitted to go into York, or no—the reason given for their detention is the intended attack to be made on that town by the Americans, as soon as the French arrive to block up the Harbour.

NOV: 5TH. After the capture of Stony Point, the rebels evacuated it, and our troops again took possession. By late accounts, our people have blown up the fortifications erected by them on the North River—and have all retired to New York.

NOV: 10TH. Our troops have evacuated Rhode Island[1] (after having kept possession three years against the united attempts of France and America) and are retir'd to York. Various are the conjectures on this manœuvre—for my own part it is beyond my comprehension. However it has answered one purpose, that of putting these rascals in great spirits, who

---

[1] In October 1779 Clinton decided to concentrate all troops in the northern colonies at New York. He was in great need of reinforcements for the protection of the West Indies. Rhode Island had been occupied in December 1776.

say our troops are recall'd and we are going to leave the continent.

Nov: 12th. A small party of our troops having made an incursion into the Jerseys—and destroy'd a magazine—in their retreat the Commanding Officer, Lieut Col: Simcoe, was wounded and taken.

Nov: 15th. The French and Americans after a few days open trenches before the town of Savannah, storm'd our works at different quarters—but were repulsed. Their loss is said to be considerable; amongst the slain is Count Pulaski,[1] and amongst the wounded Count d'Estaing, who has re-embarked all his troops, and gone as it is supposed to the West Indies. The Americans have cross'd the Savannah river and retir'd to South Carolina.

Nov: 18th. Sir Henry Clinton with 10,000 men is reported to have embark'd at York on a secret expedition—suppos'd for the subjection of South Carolina.

Nov: 21st. A strange meteor was seen in the south, just as the sun went down. It appear'd like a ball of fire and left a long trail of light—something like the turnings of a cork screw—visible for near an hour.

Nov: 25th. The first fall of snow for this season—it is two feet deep.

Nov: 30th. Being St Andrew's Day, several of our Caledonian lads met at a tavern. Some Americans being there a quarrel ensued on some trifling subject, and a rebel captain struck one of our officers—who immediately challeng'd him. Instead of accepting it the Son of Liberty only abus'd them

---

[1] One of the young foreign officers, chiefly French and Polish, idealists and adventurers, who crossed the sea to serve in the American forces. Another volunteer of the same kind was the Marquis de La Fayette.

the more and swore he would get them put into gaol. Brown was unfortunately in the fray.

DECEMBER 1ST. The officers in the riot of yesterday are confin'd to their rooms till Mr Atlee (who is at present in Philadelphia) returns—when the affair is to be brought to a hearing and settled.

DEC: 7TH. To such a low state is got the credit of Congress money that our messman says he can provide us no longer, though we pay him weekly 50 pounds each—for dinner alone, without drink.

DEC: 10TH. No tavern keeper choosing to mess us 'for paper, we were obliged to break up. My landlord offering to provide me dinner for 2 shill: and 6 pence silver daily, I have accepted it. My expenses at present are above two guineas weekly and this at a time when I am reduced to half pay by the neglect of those who ought to supply me with cash— a comfortable situation.

DEC: 12TH. Washington, thinking the southern Colonies in danger, had detach'd three thousand of his best troops to assist them. Am in hopes they will arrive too late as they have a march of 700 miles before they arrive at the scene of action— a jaunt not the most desirable at any time, much less so when the ground is covered with snow.

DEC: 14TH. A remarkable cold thick snow-storm.

DEC: 20TH. Genl Gates pass'd through here in his way to the south'ard—where it is imagin'd he is to command. Gates was dress'd in a grey frock coat and a bob-wig—his suite was two aide de camps and a domestick.

DEC: 25TH. There being no other place of public worship (where they preacht in English) but a Roman Catholic chapel, went there—but the cold was so intense that I was almost froze before service was over. Something very extraordinary, but most of the Roman Catholics are friends to Government and I believe, if an opportunity offered, would fight against those of their own religion—the French.

DEC: 29TH. The 17th Regt were brought here under a guard and are to be sent to Virginia—the poor fellows are ragged and the weather piercing cold.

## Anno Domini—1780

JANUARY 1ST. New Year's Day—the third since my captivity and no more prospect of an exchange now than at the first. The people have a custom of welcoming in the New Year by firing of muskets; they kept such a clattering all last night that I imagin'd an enemy had attacked the town—or that the inhabitants were gone mad.

JAN: 5TH. 150 more of British prisoners came here, but the guard are so averse to marching in this weather that they have refus'd taking further charge of our men—40 of whom have already made their escape.

JAN: 7TH. Two Regts of Virginians whose time of enlistment is expir'd march'd through without arms (in their way home); both battalions scarcely muster 200 men, and they made the most rueful tattered figure I ever have seen. If this is the reward of your services, and gratitude of your country, deluded Americans—your situations are not enviable.

JAN: 9TH. The guard which brought our 150 men on the 5th were prevail'd on again to take charge of them—when they march'd, only 50 remain'd.

JAN: 11TH. A Regt of Continentals[1]—part of the reinforcement for the security of the Southern States—march'd in here. They were 450 strong, had good clothing, were well arm'd and show'd more of the military in their appearance than I ever conceived American troops had yet attain'd.

JAN: 12TH. The troops which march'd in to town yesterday are not under the strictest subordination—they refus'd

[1] The 'Continental army' was a new levy, raised by Washington during the winter of 1777-8. Trained by an efficient German officer, Steuben, their skill and discipline were unprecedented among American troops.

[ 79 ]

pursuing their route today on account of the cold weather. Their officers do not seem capable of obliging them.

JAN: 13TH. Genl Thompson arriv'd last night from Philadelphia and assures us that an exchange is positively agreed to; this has put us in high glee.

JAN: 15TH. The Mohairs (aliter Town Bucks) having hinted at giving balls—at which no British officers were to be invited—it was resolv'd to be beforehand with them; gave a hop last night at which all the ladies in town were present. It was an agreeable evening—had a supper and danced till three this morning.

A great altercation this even between the men and officers of the Continental Regt—it rose to such a pitch that the men swore they would not march and call'd their Col: a d—nd rebel rascal.

JAN: 17TH. The officers have at length got the better of the men and the Regiment marched this morn with the most refractory in irons.

JAN: 18TH. A most shocking murder was committed last night near this town by some drunken rascals—by way of a frolic. A country man coming into the room where they were drinking, he was desir'd to play cards—with which he complied, but having lost some money he declin'd playing any more. This refusal exasperated the villains and one proposed roasting him, which they perform'd by the most cruel methods they could devise—till at last they burnt him to death over a red-hot stove.

JAN: 19TH. A Regt of 400 men with six pieces of brass cannon march'd in great parade into the town—the cannon are some of those taken from Burgoyne. The troops were well cloth'd and are a part of the southern reinforcement. They have 3 standards, one in the centre of the Regt, and one in the middle of each wing; the colours were blue, red and white, with thirteen stripes in the corner of each.

JAN: 21ST. Not a farthing in my pocket, do not know where to apply for any loan and thirty guineas in debt—thanks to Loring for all this. I was going to curse thee, Joshua, but, upon recollection, thou art sufficiently curst in thy wife.

JAN: 24TH. Another Regt of 400 men pass'd through for Virginia. Have an account that two thousand rebels under Genl Stirling past over on the ice to Staten Island; our troops having notice of their approach got into their works—the rebels finding them too strong for to storm retired without effecting any thing.

JAN: 26TH. A principal inhabitant dying, was buried this even, at which I cannot help observing a custom of this country—that the body is always carried by the chief people of the town and the gentlemen look on it as the greatest mark of respect to be appointed a bearer. As the person buried was very corpulent they paid pretty dearly for their honour.

FEBRUARY 1ST. The weather is so remarkably cold that a rapid stream never known to be frozen—but in the stillest parts—is now so cover'd with ice and snow as not to be discovered from terra firma.

FEB: 4TH. Mr Cope—my landlord—was call'd before the Chief Justice for raising reports prejudicial to the United States. His principal fault was saying Charlestown was taken by the British. Cope confess'd he had spoken of it as it was the common talk—he was reprimanded for his easy belief and dismiss'd.

FEB: 5TH. Forty people crossing the Susquehanna in sleighs—being on their return from a wedding—the ice broke, and six and thirty were drowned—amongst the unfortunates the new married couple.

FEB: 6TH. Of all the situations of life, that of having no pursuit is the worst. The mind having nothing to occupy its attention falls into a lethargy which makes it grow tir'd and displeas'd with every thing about it. This is my case; my time hangs heavy and I scarcely know how to spin out the day. I generally lay till ten, go to breakfast and then down the town to play billiards or pick up the news. Here I find a number of stupid beings as dull as myself—yawning and sauntering from room to room and cursing their ill stars for keeping them in such a vile hole as Lancaster. After satisfying my curiosity as to news and having vented my spleen either by swearing at the weather or times, I return home better pleas'd for finding that I am not the only phlegmatic creature of the society; and with a great deal of ado drawl out the remainder of the day talking politicks with my landlord, nonsense with the young lady of the house (a good agreeable girl) or building castles in the air which, when vanish'd, serve by comparison to make my present existence more disagreeable. What an opportunity to study French or some other useful language, but it is impossible to procure books.

FEB: 8TH. A day capable to make an Englishman hang himself—the wind howls discord and it snows so hard that one would think it intended to cover us. Not a soul is stirring through the streets and were it not for half a dozen brats squalling and fighting in the next room, I could almost imagine myself in a town just after Noah's Flood. Mem: just reading the Bible.

FEB: 11TH. Congress have issued orders that no prisoner of war shall be exchanged till his debts are paid—this is a good sign and I hope a prelude to a general cartel. A number of letters were sent from York to the officers here—none for any of our Regt. I am afraid we have been so long absent, that our friends have forgot us.

FEB: 13TH. Rain—a sure indication of the winter breaking up. I am happy at it, having just heard an exchange is agreed on and is positively to take place as soon as the weather will permit the marching of prisoners. If this proves an humbug— am determin'd never to think there is a probability of an exchange till I enter New York.

FEB: 17TH. Received information that an officer is coming from York with clothing and money for the prisoners— I hope it is true. Our people have been shockingly neglectful of us, and were it not that our enemies have more compassion than our friends, we might have been starv'd ere now.

FEB: 20TH. Alarm'd today by an officer coming with a party of men—who has orders to carry all the prisoners of war to Frederick Fort, Maryland; the most dismal place, by the description, that can be imagin'd, it being environ'd by a pine swamp. Our Commissary imagines it a mistake and that it is only meant to remove the private men. An express was sent to Philadelphia this morn for an explanation of the orders, till whose return we shall be a little anxious, as it is certainly better to stay here than travel 150 miles for a worse situation—besides we have no money and are greatly in debt.

FEB: 24TH. A duel was fought this morning between Mr Carey and Mr Swords (two of us). After discharging pistols without effect the seconds interfered and it was made up—it was occasion'd by a drunken quarrel in which blows past.

FEB: 26TH. The officer who was sent out of York (and who was reported to have brought clothing and money for all the prisoners) has only brought two small trunks—one for Col: Johnson and the other for a Mr Duncanson. The mountain has brought forth a mouse. Am not much deceiv'd —my surprise would have been greater had clothing and money really been sent; that would have been entirely contrary to the plan our friends have adopted, who seem to think a prisoner beneath their consideration and leave him to buffet against poverty, contempt and rags—till such time as they find it convenient to exchange him.

FEB: 28TH. Several officers, being a little merry last night, sung God save the King—for which they were threatened to be put into prison this morning. The great ones have thought better of it and we are only ordered never to be guilty of the like again for fear of the consequences—but we are determin'd to sing it whenever we choose in defiance of all the gaols and rebels in America.

MARCH 3RD. The landing of the British troops (under Sir Henry Clinton) in Georgia is confess'd by Congress but as usual to palliate the impending evil they have sunk a number of ships by storms and drown'd half the army.

MARCH 6TH. The spring is advancing rapidly and the feather'd gentry who forsake this country and fly south'ard during the frozen months are again return'd and chant harmony from every budding bush.

MARCH 10TH. The people are perfectly enraged at the heavy taxes and a militia law that is about to pass—by which every person between the ages of 60 and 16, who refuses turning out when call'd on, confiscates estates and property. This last has incens'd some towns so much that they sent a remonstrance begging it may be dropp'd—at the head of which (in terrorem) was depicted a bloody tomahawk.

MARCH 11TH About 70 of our private men were sent off for Fort Frederick—the account of our going there was a mistake.

MARCH 12TH. Troops are marching from all quarters towards the south'ard. A party of horse pass'd through to day and more are expected—imagine they are in trepidation for the Carolinas.

MARCH 20TH. American papers mentions Sir Henry Clinton and our army taking possession of James's Island—within 2 miles of Charlestown—by good intelligence. The place is strongly fortified, has a numerous garrison under a Genl Lincoln and intends to make a stout defence.

APRIL 7TH. Heard of an engagement between our Fleet, who were bound for the relief of Gibraltar,[1] and the Spaniards. It was fought near the Gut—Sir George Bridges Rodney who commanded ours was victorious and took or destroy'd 8 sail of the line; amongst the taken was the Spanish admiral.

APRIL 18TH. A large reinforcement of troops are embarked from York to join Sir Henry Clinton, who has begun the siege of Charlestown. A number of Americans have enter'd the town since our troops took post near it.

MAY 2ND. Nature is now in its gayest apparel, every thing being in bloom. This town from the mode of laying it out—by which every house is allow'd a garden—appears to be situated in a wilderness of fruit trees whose diversity of bloom blended—and interrupted by houses, churches etc. etc.—forms altogether a most enchanting scene.

[1] Rodney, on his way to take up the West Indian command, was ordered to relieve Gibraltar, besieged by the Spaniards. This he achieved by the defeat of the Spanish Fleet, in a night action off Cape St Vincent (January 1780).

MAY 10TH. The Indians are on the frontiers and seldom a day passes that does not bring accounts of their depredations. At present there are affairs of too great moment on the carpet to think of resenting their inroads, so they scalp and burn with impunity.

MAY 16TH. The most recent accounts from South Carolina mentions Charlestown being so closely invested by land and water that no intelligence of the situation of the garrison could be receiv'd. Our ships have enter'd the harbour in spite of their shipping and Fort Moultrie—which the rebels thought impossible. The only thing to hinder the town falling into our hands will be the climate. If the siege is protracted till next month, the heat will be too intense for the soldiers to carry on the approaches.

MAY 23RD. The Americans are in great spirits, as they say several thousand French are coming to join Washington's Army—sent across the Atlantic by their great and good ally to assist them.

JUNE 1ST. An engagement has been fought in the West Indies between the English Fleet—under Sir George Rodney—and the French under Count d'Estaing.[1] Our accounts are so various that it is impossible to say who came off victorious. The French have taken Grenada and St Vincent.

JUNE 3RD. For these two days past the rebels have landed ten thousand French troops at the Hook near New York but in their last paper they say it was premature.

JUNE 6TH. Charlestown is taken—it surrendered the 12th of May. What number of prisoners were captured is uncertain;

[1] The French Commander was now not, as Hughes says, d'Estaing, but the more able de Guichen.

[ 86 ]

Whigs make out militia, Continental and sailors about 5 thousand—the Tories ten thousand men.

JUNE 11TH. Our people have flung a bridge of boats across the small arm of the sea which separates Staten Island from the Province of New Jersey and cross'd six thousand men under Lieut Genl Kniphausen—who has taken post at Elizabethtown. This movement has put the whole country in commotion and all the militia are ordered out. It is said our troops destroy the houses of the militia who take up arms but those who remain at home have their property secur'd—the most politic plan our Genls have yet fallen on and the surest method of finishing the war.

JUNE 15TH. The Congress have thought proper to acknowledge the loss of Charlestown[1]—they make the number of Continental troops taken 2600 but say nothing of militia or sailors. They confess (for the first time) that the British behaved with humanity to the captives.

JUNE 20TH. A complaint having been lodg'd against one of our officers for speaking disrespectfully of the militia's martial appearance, he was call'd before the Commissary to answer for his conduct—Col: Johnson and several others went with him. At their arrival at Mr Atlee's, they found that diminutive gentleman in a violent rage which he vented on them in most opprobious language; but the storm soon expending he grew asham'd of his behaviour and to mollify us extended our parole three miles.

JUNE 23RD. Sir Henry Clinton is return'd to New York with the British Grenadiers and some other troops; the rest of the army employ'd at the siege of Charlestown is left under the

---

[1] In May 1780 General Benjamin Lincoln surrendered Charlestown and an army of about 6000 men to Clinton.

Earl of Cornwallis to perfect the reduction of South Carolina. His Lordship is now in full march for Camden where it is imagin'd he will be join'd by vast numbers of Loyalists. During the siege we had scarcely 200 men killed and wounded.

JUNE 26TH. About 100 militia of this town march'd for camp—in passing by some of us, who were observing them, they honour'd us with the appellation of Bloody Backs. Lt Horndon was beat publickly in the streets this morn by the adjutant of the militia for using freedoms with that gentleman's wife—Atlee will not interfere in the quarrel so Horndon must put up with the drubbing.

JUNE 27TH. Went with some ladies on an excursion into the country; in our tour hearing by accident of a wedding within 5 miles of us, nothing would please the girls but we must be there. We arriv'd just as the ceremony began, and were ushered into a large room where near 50 people were seated at two long tables. At the head of the room stood two old men who pray'd alternately, to appearance extempore, but it being in German I could not understand them. After long praying mixed with long pauses, the couple were brought in the middle of the floor, when the old men gave them good advice as to their future behaviour and asked if they were willing to live together—on their assenting their hands were join'd and the affair was finish'd. It was now about 12 o'clock —the tables were immediately spread and we had an excellent German repast (where every thing was boiled and roasted to rags) with plenty of cyder, toddy and beer. After the appetite was satisfied, the whole company adjourn'd to an extensive lawn where the young men and women play'd at various games till 4 o'clock, when we receiv'd notice that the dinner was ready. This meal was a profusion of soups, meats, pies, &c, enough for a Regt of soldiers. The attendants were the bridegroom and his men; the bride, who was remarkably pretty, did the honours of the table supported by her maids. The signal for the whole being over—and after which people depart without ceremony—is the handing a plate round the table in which every person puts what they think proper; this is suppos'd to be a gratification to the cooks for their trouble. These people are of a sect call'd Mennonite. I could never gain a perfect knowledge of their tenets—I believe they approach nearest the Quakers; like them they think it unlawful to fight, or pay taxes, and they never wear buckles or metal buttons. There are numbers of these people in this part of the country who are rich farmers. This wedding was esteemed a very poor one—they sometimes have 500 guests. Our party turn'd out very entertaining—though in leaping I was unfortunately thrown, and the horse stumbled over me; receiv'd but little hurt.

JUNE 28TH. An action has happened in the Jerseys, in which our troops (as the rebels say) by the superiority of numbers gain'd their point which was the burning of Springfield—after which they return'd to Elizabethtown and from thence crossed to Staten Island taking up the bridge of boats which they had flung across to keep up the communication. A very pretty expedition: six thousand men having penetrated 12 miles into the country—burnt a village and returned.

JULY 1ST. A party of 400 Americans under a Col: Burford have been entirely cut off by Col: Tarleton, who was sent in pursuit of them by the Earl of Cornwallis with a detachment of 300 Light Horse and Light Infantry. The affair happened at King's Mountain,[1] Carolina. Col: Burford and 30 men were all that escaped—a great number of waggons loaded with different stores fell into the conquerors' possession.

JULY 3RD. The prospect of the ensuing harvest is very promising. Rye is already fit for cutting; currants, rasberries and cherries are so plenty that you get them for nothing amongst the farmers.

JULY 4TH. A great day—being the third anniversary of American Independence; the militia fired thirteen rounds and we had nothing but bon-fires and rejoicings all night.

JULY 6TH. Receiv'd a bill for three months pay from New York.

JULY 9TH. One of our officers being refused leave to go a few miles out of his limits, took pique—and flung up his parole. He is in gaol and closely confined.

JULY 11TH. The German officers who have been our companions for two years past were sent off to Reading—the reason given for their removal is their having advised the German farmers (settled round here) not to pay their taxes.

The officer who flung up his parole in a pet, in three days confinement has thought better of it and has now requested liberty to come out of gaol again. He is universally con-demn'd for having acted a most foolish part—he ought either to have stuck up to his resolve of remaining there, or not gone at all.

---

[1] An American relieving force for Charlestown, under Colonel Burford, turned back on the fall of the city. Cornwallis sent Tarleton in pursuit, who, overtaking Burford at Waxhaws on the North Carolina border, cut his force to pieces. At King's Mountain (30 miles away) in the following October, Colonel Ferguson, detached by Cornwallis to organise a 'resist-ance movement' in the western part of the Carolinas, was pinned down by a locally-raised opposition and annihilated. (See p. 99.)

JULY 14TH. Another of our officers was sent to gaol for propagating humbugs (aliter telling lies) amongst the country-people.

JULY 15TH. An order from the Board of War that every British officer should wear his proper uniform and that whoever after this was found in a coloured coat should be taken up and put into prison. This has put most of us to an inconveniency as it is amazing difficult to procure cloth.

JULY 17TH. We have certain intelligence of the arrival of a French Fleet with a number of troops at Newport,[1] Rhode Island, but report has not yet ascertain'd their strength and numbers. All the horses in the country are collecting for their use—it is imagined they are immediately to cooperate with Washington's forces.

JULY 20TH. Admiral Graves is arrived at York with five sail of the line. It is said that he fell in with the French and had a smart brush with them prior to their arrival at Rhode Island. An express pass'd through with despatches for Genl Gates—which (from good authority) I hear contain orders for that Genl to collect the troops and militia of the Southern States and attack Lord Cornwallis, whose progress has alarmed the continent.

JULY 25TH. Three other unfortunate fellows who were taken at sea came here on parole.

JULY 27TH. The report of the day is that Admiral Arbuthnot with 10 sail of the line and Sir Henry Clinton with 8 thousand men—are gone to attack Rhode Island.

---

[1] The French had in May dispatched a reinforcement of 6000 troops to Rhode Island, which neither Clinton, nor Rodney, on his arrival in September, felt strong enough to dislodge.

JULY 29TH. Several prisoners made their escape last night —some officers' servants are confined for having assisted them.

AUGUST 2ND. Three of our bucks got so drunk in the country that in returning to town they fell off their horses and were very near killing themselves—one of them is at present in so bad a way that his recovery is doubtful. So much for drinking and buckism—it is too warm to live with comfort.

AUGT 5TH. Two of our officers being exchanged we took the opportunity of sending a memorial to Sir Henry Clinton informing him of our long captivity and begging to be included in the first cartel. Some rascals pelted me with brick-bats this even—luckily escaped unhurt.

AUGT 8TH. The best information concerning the French makes them 8 sail of the line and four thousand men—they are fortifying Newport Harbour very strongly. Admiral Arbuthnot with the British Fleet is cruising off Rhode Island.

AUGT 11TH. Washington has crossed the North River and taken post at the White Plains where he has called on the militia of the Northern States to join him, with an intent to attack New York. They make his army already 30,000 strong.

AUGT 12TH. An express arrived here from Washington with a circulary letter to the different towns, in which that general requests their sending three classes of militia immediately to him—which if they perform with alacrity, he promises never to trouble them more, as he has now an opportunity of finishing the war. This shows that the military ardour of the country is greatly lessen'd when Washington himself is oblig'd to make use of so poor a stratagem to engage the people to assist him. I have it from good authority that Washington's real (or what the rebels call their standing) army is reduced to 4000 men.

AUGT 16TH. The Indians are come down in great numbers on the frontiers where they have taken some forts, carried off the people and destroy'd the country.

AUGT 20TH. The attack on New York is now blown over. It seems that when Washington call'd on the militia, Sir H. Clinton had left York with the best part of his army and was on his way to Rhode Island; but hearing of the rebels' plan he return'd and frustrated their intent. Washington has again cross'd the North River and got into his strong holds; Sir Henry has encamped at Whitestone Bay, Long Island—about 25 miles from York.

AUGT 22ND. An English packet being taken with five officers on board, they were all sent here. By them we have accounts of a terrible riot in London[1]—raised by that madman Lord George Gordon—in which many of the mobile were killed; but not till they had raised to such an insolent pitch of fury that they set fire to several parts of the metropolis, when the military power was called on, which with some exertion stopped the further proceeding of the vagabond gentry. Ld G. Gordon is confined in the Tower and it is said will be tried for high treason.

AUGT 25TH. 16 of our men who were in the prison broke through the wall and made their escape—in order to drown the noise of their working, they pretended to be very merry on some good news they had heard.

AUGT 26TH. Three classes of the militia are again ordered out, but for what particular business I cannot learn—those who refuse are fined 600 pounds. It is impossible to imagine a more abject race than the generality of these Americans. They all plainly see how much they are imposed on and say

[1] The Gordon Riots, June 1780.

themselves they shall be ruined if the war last—and yet they have not spirit to rise and turn out those rascals at the head of their government; instead of which they all grumble, and when the tax-gatherers come round, though many refuse paying they allow them to take what they please (which is always three times the value of the tax), and thus by ruining themselves think they do a meritorious act and call themselves friends to the British.

AUGT 30TH. Heard by accident from Capt: Lyman that my sister Eliza was married to a Mr Stanhope.

SEPTEMBER 2ND. Genl Gates, who for two months past has been collecting the forces of the Southern States, having approacht Ld Cornwallis, a general action ensued near Camden[1] which terminated in a total defeat to the rebel army. Report says the Americans had one thousand killed and two thousand wounded or taken; Gates himself was pursued 25 miles and never stopt till he got 120 miles from the field of action, where he is again collecting the fugitives.

SEPT: 5TH. The militia who have been twice call'd on are again ordered home. The rebel leaders appear a good deal confus'd and I believe do not know what plan to fall on to keep up their adherents' spirits. May Discord prevail in their councils and Timidity fall on their troops!

SEPT: 9TH. Commissioners are appointed to settle an exchange—on our part Genl Phillips, on the American Genl Lincoln. I put no confidence in the negotiation—if it does succeed it will be an agreeable surprise.

---

[1] The defeat of the American counter-attack in the Carolinas. Cornwallis completely defeated Gates who was advancing with much superior forces upon him. Gates was then superseded by Nathaniel Greene, the most able American general after Washington himself.

SEPT: 10TH. A French recruiting party is at present beating up in this town for Hussars (or Light Horse); they offer twenty guineas bounty. An American party who were here lately gave six guineas at enlistment and a promise of 300 acres of land at the conclusion of the war. They pickt up 14 men out of this town, mostly deserters—there are above a thousand German deserters settled at different farm houses within 30 miles of this town.

SEPT: 14TH. Congress have thought proper to give a lame account of the late engagement to the south'ard[1] but they neither give the force or loss of either party. They ascribe their defeat to the cowardice of their militia who ran at the first fire. In a Baltimore paper they say Ld Cornwallis's army consisted of eighteen hundred regulars and two thousand four hundred friends to Government. I am glad to hear them confess that we have so great a body of their countrymen in the field against them.

SEPT: 16TH. A detachment of British troops have attacked the Spanish settlements in South America and it is said have been joined by numbers of the Mexicans who wanted to shake off the Spanish yoke—this will be a proper punishment for Spain's perfidy.

SEPT: 18TH. Remarkable for nothing but the anniversary of my captivity—having been three years a prisoner.

SEPT: 23RD. Sir G. Rodney is arrived at New York with ten sail of the line from the West Indies. Various are our conjectures on this manœuvre but the generality seem to think our people intend to attack the French at Rhode Island.

SEPT: 26TH. The Indians have committed such outrages in the back countries and are in such force that the whole

[1] I.e. Camden.

country are in alarm. A detachment from Canada have taken Fort Anne and Fort George and carried off their garrisons.

SEPT: 29TH. The people are much alarmed at the defection of Genl Arnold[1] who is reported to have gone to New York and joined our troops. The story told on this occasion is this— Arnold has long carried on a private correspondence with Sir H. Clinton, at the conclusion of which he agreed to deliver up West Point Fort (on the North River), where he commanded, to the British. Two or three days before the plot was to take place Arnold requested an intelligence officer might be sent him (in disguise) for the more perfect settling the scheme of operation, and to prevent mistakes in the execution. Major I. André went and concluded the business but unfortunately in returning poor André was taken by three militia men and papers found on him disclosing the whole affair. Arnold hearing of André's capture made his escape to one of our ships of war which lay near his post. It is imagined André will be hanged for a spy.

OCTOBER 3RD. Arnold's flight is certainly true. The affair was so well concerted that Washington and le Marquis de La Fayette were to have been taken. The ship to which Arnold retired (after it was discovered) had 400 men concealed in her hold—these were to have attack'd the Fort in the night, on which Arnold would have immediately surrendered, and Sir H. Clinton had formed measures to arrive in the morning with a considerable force and confirm the possession. It is said by

---

[1] Benedict Arnold had been a brilliant leader of the Americans, in the capture of Ticonderoga, the invasion of Canada, and the defeat of Burgoyne. Out of a combination of pique and need for money he had begun to negotiate with the British. The correspondence with Clinton was conducted through his Adjutant-General, Major André, who was captured and hanged as a spy.

the rebels themselves that this stroke would have ruin'd them. Washington has offered to deliver up André for Arnold.

OCT: 7TH. Cannot procure money at the exorbitant premium of 50 pr cent; I owe near 50 guineas, have not a shilling in my purse and cannot borrow sixpence—a pretty situation when joined to that of being a prisoner. I believe even Job would lose his patience, to be in my circumstances.

OCT: 10TH. Major André was certainly hanged on the 2nd of this month. He died with such fortitude that it has drawn the admiration of his foes. When asked at the gallows if he had anything to say, he express'd a wish that his death had been more honourable, But Gentlemen, adds he (speaking to the rebel officers who stood round him), as that wish is futile and my request of being shot (for politick ends) has been denied— I call on you all to bear witness that I die like a brave man. Then with an unmoved countenance he tyed a handkerchief over his eyes—and put the cord round his neck. He was dress'd in full regimentals and was executed pursuant to the sentence of a Court Martial compos'd of general officers. Thus has a man universally beloved by all that knew him and publickly esteemed by all that heard of him, endowed with great natural parts, improved by education and travel and who from his youth (being only five or six and twenty) promis'd to make a distinguished figure in the military line, fallen a victim and graced the triumph of bloody, unjust, and unnatural rebellion—cut off too by an ignominious death (if that can be call'd ignominy to die in an attempt to serve his country and King). He was Adjutant General, chief aide de camp to Sir H. Clinton and a major of Foot.

OCT: 12TH. One of our officers turn'd mad and jumpt into the water to drown himself—being suspected he had been followed by two officers who just came time enough to save him.

OCT: 14TH. One Reed, the titular governor of the Province, arrived here. He is on a tour to investigate the state of the Colony. The people forebode no good from his visit as it seems he does not think them taxed sufficiently—this town raises 100,000 pounds yearly.

OCT: 17TH. The Indians still continuing troublesome, the first class or company of every battalion are ordered to garrison the most exposed towns. Those belonging to this town marched this morn—N.B. the militia are divided into eight classes.

OCT: 19TH. The Commissioners who met to settle an exchange are again broke up without coming to any thing. Morgan, with 400 rifle men, has been detached by Washington to the assistance of the Southern States; Gates is not to be again employ'd, as it is said he misbehaved in the last action.

OCT: 21ST. The report of this day entirely contradicts that of the 19th; for they now say that the Commissioners have settled the cartel and that we are already exchanged—a little time will clear up the matter. The officer who lost his senses by proper applications has recovered his reason.

OCT: 23RD. The Tories give out that two American generals and some of the Congress have deserted to New York and that Mr Laurens[1]—late President of Congress—was taken going to France and all his papers secured, which has given our Ministry an insight to all their private negotiations.

OCT: 25TH. We had bonfires and great rejoicings last night

[1] Henry Laurens, President of the Continental Congress. He left for Holland in August 1780 and was taken at sea. His papers revealed the existence of negotiations with the Dutch. This precipitated the actual declaration of war with Holland in December 1780.

—occasioned by the news of a victory gained over a detachment of our troops in South Carolina.[1] The rebels say we lost 1000 men.

OCT: 31ST. Thunder, lightning and hail storm—followed by a deep snow.

NOVEMBER 3RD. Three thousand British troops are landed at Portsmouth, Virginia, under the command of Brigadier Genl Leslie.

NOV: 7TH. Received a bill of 3 months pay from York and at the same time a letter informing us of an exchange being agreed to.

NOV: 10TH. A party of 150 horse came in ⟨to⟩ town this morn and in the evening 150 Light Infantry—their route is to Carolina.

NOV: 14TH. Some of the American officers calling the 17th Regt, who were taken at Stony Point, a parcel of cowards, it was near producing a general duel; but the Americans apologising for the expression and attributing it to their being drunk, the affair terminated.

NOV: 18TH. Col: Skinner—an American Commissary—arrived with the agreeable intelligence of our being all to be exchanged, and tells us we may go off for New York when it suits our conveniency and we can get our debts settled—this last will give me some trouble.

NOV: 19TH. Several officers having settled their affairs departed this morn. I shall esteem myself lucky to get off in three days.

NOV: 21ST. Have settled my affairs by drawing a bill on New York at 12 pr cent discount. Caleb Cope (my landlord)

[1] Ferguson's defeat at King's Mountain (see note on p. 90) which did much to offset American gloom over Camden.

insisted on treating me with wine this even—as it was to be my last night; but his head being weak the juice of the grape has been too powerful for Caleb's spirit.

Nov: 22nd. Left Lancaster in company with Brown; Cope (mine host) insisted on seeing us six miles in our way which contrary to our desire he performed. We are on foot with a servant carrying our road apparel in a knapsack. Our parole extends to Elizabethtown where we are to deliver ourselves up to a Major Adams—the rebel Commissary. We began our journey a little after 12 o'clock and before 5 had reacht Adamstown, which is 21 mile—put up for the night at a small tavern with good accommodations, and a civil landlord, though a great rebel.

Nov: 23rd. Breakfasted where we lay and paid pretty dear for our landlord's civility. At 9 o'clock sallied forth, but the roads being bad, on account of a great rain last night, it was 12 before we reacht Reading. The German officers press'd us to dine with them, their dinner being just ready; we excused ourselves and after taking a slight refreshment at an inn proceeded on our walk. At a lonely public house 11 miles from Reading put up for the evening. Our host is a Dutchman and the most laughable droll fellow I ever met. He gives us the best his house affords—which is no great things.

Nov: 24th. A frost. March'd 8 miles before breakfast and 14 after—lay within 3 miles of Allentown. The roads are frozen so hard that my feet are swell'd with walking and are become very painful. Got good accommodations and civil people.

Nov: 25th. So stiff and my feet so sore that I travelled in the utmost pain. Went to Bethlehem (9 miles) before breakfast and to Easton (12 miles farther) after—the last walk in a hard rain which has crippled me and I can proceed no farther till my legs are better. We have overtaken here several officers who left Lancaster the day before us; am at present in my old lodgings.

Nov: 26th. Remained at Easton. A man was hanged this morning for piloting some people through the back woods, to the Indians. He was very old and has left a wife and 9 children. His death was chiefly owing to his being a noted friend to Government.

Nov: 27th. Though I can scarcely crawl, I made shift to march 21 mile. In the evening reacht Grandines (a friend); were treated with great hospitality—there were several young ladies in the house but I was not in a situation to relish their company, having by pain and fatigue walked myself into a fever.

Nov: 28th. Our landlord would receive no payment and even press'd us to remain. We departed, and I hobbled to Bound Brook (26 miles). Were civilly treated though the house was crowded on account of a great law suit in agitation; three justices gave us their room (the best in the house) for our accommodation. This is but a small town but situated in a fertile part of the Jerseys.

Nov: 29th. Marched 22 miles to Elizabethtown. Never was a person more rejoiced at the end of a journey, for I do not think it possible for me to have held out another day. Gave our pass to Major Adams who informed us that a flag of truce had just sailed for New York and that we must remain here till it returns. This gives me the less uneasiness as we are in a good tavern and our landlord (who is a physician) has plenty of books.

Nov: 30th. No news of a flag. An American officer introduced himself to me and requested my conveying a letter of the utmost consequence to our Adjt Genl at York. I undertook the affair but refused giving a receipt for it which he desired; by what I can find he is one of our spies—and a captain in the rebel service.

December 1st. Col: Skinner came here and we dined together. He tells us if a flag does not arrive tomorrow, we may cross to Staten Island in a fisherman's canoe (our people having destroyed all their boats). This offer we have accepted. The baggage and all the officers' servants arrived this evening; we give 16 guineas pr load for 150 miles.

Dec: 2nd. No flag. Paid our bill which amounted to eight pounds fifteen shillings in solid coin and cross'd in a canoe to Staten Island. After walking two or three miles reacht our advanced post where we were stop'd and, though it was just sundown, the Officer Commanding obliged Brown to go to Genls Patterson's and Skinner's quarters—a tramp of 10 miles. They excused me on account of my lameness, and by their direction I got a lodging and procured a good supper by the time Brown return'd.

Dec: 3rd. Breakfasted where we lay. The people were so civil that they would not permit us to pay any thing, though they kept tavern. In our walk to the ferry we had an opportunity of viewing two forts situated on eminences—they are both round, double abatised and picketed. Embark'd in the King's boat for York; she being a bad sailer, we must have remain'd on the water all night had not another boat come and took us on board—what with rowing and sailing we made York about 4 o'clock in the evening. Hous'd ourselves in the first inn we saw, as neither Brown or myself are in the most elegant apparel and that entirely out of vogue. Ventured to the Coffee House in the evening and found most of the lads who had arrived before us; they give unfavourable accounts of the extravagance of this place, as they say it is impossible to live under a guinea pr day—a pretty situation for Brown and me; both purses joined would not show ten shillings. We must trust to Providence.

DEC: 4TH. Went to Head Quarters and delivered the letter I received at Elizabethtown to the Adjutant Genl. He was very polite and attentive but cannot say so much for the aide de camps who were very merry on my unfashionable appearance.

DEC: 6TH. Applied to Sir Henry Clinton for cash, it being impossible for to get out of my present house till I procure some.

DEC: 7TH. The Barrackmaster gave me a billet on a house in which there are but four rooms and five families inhabit them. The poor people are in such sad circumstances that I cannot think of adding to their distress by turning any of them out. Ask'd for a new billet.

DEC: 8TH. The town is so crowded that I cannot procure any other than my first quarter. The Barrackmaster sent an assistant to turn out the people, which would have been done had I not said I would abide the loss and procure a lodging for myself.

DEC: 9TH. Went to Mr Porteous a very civil merchant and procured (on credit) a few things to appear decent. Applied for leave to go to England and join my Regt in Canada with the first fleet in the spring—no answer.

DEC: 11TH. Receiv'd some cash; paid my landlord the devil of a bill and retired with Brown to his quarters in order to live as cheap as possible.

DEC: 13TH. Borrowed money enough to answer the bill I was obliged to draw before I left Lancaster, and lodged it with Mr Watson to whom it is to be presented.

DEC: 15TH. The tailor for making charges more than the things cost first—by which means a plain suit of red stands me in 12£. How subalterns live in this hole I can't imagine.

DEC: 17TH. Two thousand men under Genl Arnold embarked for a private expedition. Arnold is much taken notice of—is made a Brigadier Genl and is now raising a corps. At his first coming in he was granted two thousand guineas for his private purse and 1600 for the furniture of a house. Met Simcoe—he was glad to see me. Simcoe embarks with his corps and is to be under Arnold—it is imagined they are to establish a post at Portsmouth, Virginia.

DEC: 20TH. Several of my old friends (the Conventioners) arrived here—they are included in the present cartel. The packet sailed for England; we have received no answer to our memorial about going to Great Britain.

DEC: 23RD. Waited on Genl Phillips who informed me I might go home if I chose and that a transport should be provided for me.

DEC: 25TH. Wiseman came in from the rebels. We have still three officers of the 53rd remaining in captivity, viz. Houghton, Mure and Digby. Christmas Day, but I cannot say a merry one.

DEC: 26TH. They say the rebels intend taking off the Commander in Chief, who lives close on the North River—Sir Henry is a little alarmed on this occasion and keeps double guards at his house, which is within pistol shot of the North Battery.

## December 1780

DEC: 28TH. Nothing stirring in this town more than if it was profound peace; the only thing we hear of is excursions by small parties of refugees who generally return with cattle and prisoners. Washington and his army are retired to winter quarters above West Point—on Hudson River—with an intent (as 'tis reported) of covering an expedition against St Johns, Canada, to be undertaken when the lakes are frozen— a perilous attempt and which I can hardly imagine will be put in execution.

## Anno Domini—1781

JANUARY 1ST. Laid up by a great cold and tooth-ache. A very pleasant day and so warm that every house have the windows open. The prospect of my affairs have brightened a little since this time last year as I am no longer in captivity— in other respects much of a sameness.

JAN: 2ND. A Court of Enquiry has been on Col: Johnston for the loss of Stony Point but that not proving satisfactory Col: Johnston demanded a Court Martial which began today.

JAN: 4TH. An account having been received of a great mutiny[1] in the rebel army, Sir H. Clinton went with the Grenadiers, Light Infantry and other troops to Staten Island in order to seize any favourable opportunity of dividing or attacking the mutineers, who are reported to amount to three thousand. These revolters have taken an advantageous post in the Jerseys, have appointed a Genl to command them named Williams (formerly a sergt in our service) and have already repulsed several parties sent to subdue them. The want of proper pay and clothing are the complaints of these men, and they threaten to engage on their own bottoms should not their grievances be speedily redressed.

JAN: 6TH. The departure of the Cork Fleet with which I was to have gone home is deferred so long for want of convoy that I have altered my plan of operation and now intend remaining here till spring when a fleet will be sent from hence to Canada.

JAN: 10TH. An expedition of six thousand men is said will be sent up the North River to attack West Point Fort—the

[1] In January 1781 Washington was faced with two serious mutinies, owing to the resentment felt by the troops against the ill-faith of Congress.

Pearl frigate and several transports have gone from the East into the North River which gives great probability that the report is true.

JAN: 12TH. Arnold's expedition has arrived in Virginia— Genl Leslie who went to Portsmouth some time ago with three thousand men has sailed from thence and is now on his way to Carolina to reinforce Ld Cornwallis.

JAN: 15TH. Genl Clinton has withdrawn the additional troops from Staten Island, having done nothing but sent a small detachment to Amboy which took a few prisoners.

JAN: 18TH. The Queen's birthday—the shipping and fort saluted.

JAN: 21ST. Three French ships of the line (viz two 74 and one 64) have made their escape out of Rhode Island—should they attack Arnold it may be attended with serious consequences.

JAN: 22ND. Met this morn the American officer who introduced himself to me at Elizabethtown and for whom I carried a letter to the Adjt Genl. He says an expedition was intended against Canada this winter but the extraordinary mildness of the season and the disaffection of the troops prevented its taking place. It was to have consisted of two brigades of Americans of 3000 men each and a detachment of two thousand French from Rhode Island. The greatest part of these troops were to have marched by land—a road being already cut for them; and their artillery, provision and remainder of men were to have cross'd Lake Champlain on the ice. St Johns and the shipping was the principal object— the destruction of which would give them the command of the lake and afford them an opportunity of throwing a number of men the ensuing summer into the upper parts of Canada, whilst ships and troops to be sent from France attacked Quebec early in the spring. So much for their plan—the Canadians it is said would have join'd in great numbers.

JAN: 23RD. It blew a hurricane which tore up trees, unroof'd houses and drove several vessels on shore. The storm was accompanied with snow which by the force of the wind has stuck to every part of the houses and makes a very droll appearance.

JAN: 24TH. A body of rebels made an attack on some refugees posted at Westchester; they did some damage and took a few prisoners, but the Loyalists, collecting, charged them so vigorously that they retreated with precipitation.

JAN: 25TH. Another revolt has broke out in the rebel army. They consist of about 700 men, have made the same demand as the first and have already dispers'd 500 militia who were sent to oppose their march. The former revolters, after marching through great part of the Jerseys in the style of an army, upon their reaching the banks of the Delaware disagreed amongst themselves and separated, some taking Congress' security for the payment of arrears, others returning quietly to their homes and the remainder still stubbornly rejecting every overture short of their demands.

JAN: 27TH. The rebel papers acknowledge that Arnold's detachment has done them immense mischief, he having penetrated to Richmond, Virginia, where their magazines of tobacco &c &c were kept, which he has destroyed together with the provision laid up for their Southern Army.

JAN: 28TH. The rebel chiefs having by finesse disarmed the last 700 mutineers have condemn'd 40 of them to be hanged. The first revolters are gone to different towns in

Pennsylvania, and Congress is obliged to keep large bodies of militia near them to watch their motions.

JAN: 30TH. The storm on the 23rd drove the Culloden of 74 guns on shore on Long Island, dismasted the Bedford of 74 guns and it is said the America (a 64) is lost—this is the more unfortunate as these ships had just been detached from Adml Graves's Fleet (lying in Gardiner's Bay) in quest of the three French vessels lately got out of Newport Harbour.

JAN: 31ST. Sailed 150 transports, victuallers &c &c for England; all the Convention officers lately exchanged whose Regiments are in Virginia went home in this fleet—those whose Regts are still in Canada remain here till a convoy offers for Quebec.

FEBRUARY 7TH. Our troops have received a severe check in Carolina[1] from a large body of rebels under Col: Morgan— the 7th and 71st Regts are entirely cut up. This defeat is ascribed to the ill-behaviour of Tarleton's cavalry, who ran at the first fire and left the infantry (who fought like heroes) unsupported. It is said Col: Tarleton cried at the cowardice of his men and displayed through the whole action the utmost bravery. The ill conduct of the legion is the more extraordinary as in all their former engagements they were always the first at any post of danger and were never known to give way.

Nothing of consequence during this month. The rebels talk a great deal of an expedition to take Arnold, in conjunction with the French Fleet. Arnold has fortified himself at Portsmouth but not thinking his situation very secure has demanded a reinforcement which it is said will be sent him. The dullest month in the year, as it is perpetually drizzling,

[1] The battle of Cowpens in January 1781, at which Tarleton was defeated by Morgan.

with now and then a severe snow storm. The amusements in this town are plays once a week—vilely enacted by officers—and balls once a fortnight.

MARCH 3RD. A detachment of our troops under Major Craig has taken post at Wilmington on Cape Fear River, North Carolina. Ld Cornwallis on hearing of Tarleton's defeat mounted his army on horses and pursued Morgan, who was too nimble for his Lordship and has made a good retreat with his prisoners—however our army has penetrated to the borders of Virginia. It is said the rebel Genl Greene is collecting all the forces in the Southern States and that he intends to risk a general action as nothing else can stop Cornwallis's career.

MARCH 4TH. Some French cruisers have taken the Romulus, a 44 gun ship, and carried her into Rhode Island.

MARCH 6TH. Paul Jones[1] is arrived at Philadelphia in the Ariel, of 20 guns, and it is reported that he has already quarrelled with Congress because they would not give him a larger ship which he demanded. His character for cruelty is so universally detested that all the sailors of his ship have left him and no others will serve under him.

MARCH 10TH. A large reinforcement of troops have arrived at Charlestown.

MARCH 14TH. Sir George Rodney in consequence of a Dutch war[2] has taken St Eustatia and an amazing number of shipping in the harbour; the value of this capture is said to be worth two millions sterling. This is a severe blow to the rebel

[1] The boldest of American privateers, an ex-Scottish slave-trader. He did much damage to British commerce and even raided the English coast.
See note on p. 98.

trade—St Eustatia[1] being their principal market in the West Indies.

MARCH 15TH. Genl Phillips has embarked with near 3000 men to reinforce Genl Arnold at Portsmouth, which place the French and Americans certainly intend attacking.

MARCH 16TH. The whole French Fleet have sailed from Rhode Island with a part of their troops on board. Our fleet under Adml Arbuthnot[2] has left Gardiner's Bay (having burnt the hull of the Culloden which they could not get off) and by last accounts were crowding all sail to intercept the French before they can get into Chesapeake Bay. We expect every hour news of a naval engagement; both squadrons are eight sail of the line but the number of guns in our favour.

MARCH 20TH. The Fleets met on the 16th and an engagement ensued off the Capes of Virginia but it terminated without any thing decisive—the French have given up their attack on Arnold and are on their return to Newport. Our Fleet are in the Chesapeake repairing their damages.

MARCH 26TH. The French have got back to Rhode Island with three of their ships dismasted. They acknowledge the loss of 80 men killed and 120 wounded—ours was much less.

MARCH 30TH. Have been for three days past with the British Grenadiers on Long Island—I had the pleasure of seeing them on a field day go through their manœuvres and fire ball cartridges. They are ⟨a⟩ noble set of fellows and

[1] The Dutch island of St Eustatius in the Leeward Group had been the centre of a heavy Dutch-American trade conducted under cover of Dutch neutrality.

[2] Marriot Arbuthnot, in command on the New York station at the time. The French Fleet sailed from Newport to the Chesapeake to cut off Arnold who had raided Richmond in Virginia, but was driven off.

I believe scarcely to be equalled. Both battalions form a body of 900 men—under Lt Colonels York and Fox.

APRIL 2ND. A rebel mail was brought to town which contains letters from Washington and other rebel genls describing the disaffection of their troops and the lowness of their finances. This mail with the postman was captured by one single friend to Government above 80 miles from our lines, in the most populous part of New England, and both the man and bag were brought through the country without discovery.

APRIL 5TH. Lord Cornwallis attacked Genl Greene at Guildford Court House,[1] North Carolina, on the 15th: ult: and after a severe conflict routed the rebel army and took their cannon. The British army scarcely mustered 1600 out of which it is said we had 600 killed and wounded; the Americans had near 6000 men in the field which Greene had posted in a most masterly manner—they confess the loss of about 1500 kill'd, wounded or missing.

APRIL 6TH. My brother Wm C. Hughes is appointed a capt: in the 7th Regt vice Capt: Peacock deceased—19th October 1780.

APRIL 9TH. Genl Phillips with his detachment have arrived at Portsmouth, Virginia, where a number of petty skirmishes have happened in most of which our troops were victors.

APRIL 12TH. Admiral Arbuthnot with his fleet are at present in this harbour, some of his ships being greatly in want of repair. It is publickly reported by the naval officers that in the last affair with the French there was great mismanage-

---

[1] In this engagement Cornwallis, already crippled by Tarleton's disaster at Cowpens (see p. 109) defeated a superior force under Greene, but at such cost that he could no longer oppose Greene's advance into the Carolinas.

ment—otherwise they could not have failed capturing some men of war.

APRIL 14TH. A Lieutenant of the Royal Oak was so exasperated against the Master, because he would not bear down alongside a French ship and pleaded the Adml's orders to the contrary, that he swore he would cane him the first time they were on shore; this promise he has performed by beating him publickly in the streets.

APRIL 17TH. The Confederacy—the largest frigate in the Congress service—is taken by the Roebuck (44 guns) and brought in here. She mounts 36 guns and is almost as large as one of our 60 gun ships. She struck without firing a shot.

APRIL 27TH. An expedition of two thousand men are embarked; they are supposed to be bound for Wilmington to which place Ld Cornwallis has marched for the intent of recovering his wounded. Genl Greene has taken the advantage of this movement and has again penetrated North Carolina.[1]

MAY 2ND. A Feu de joie fired in honour of Lord Cornwallis's conquest by all the troops in garrison.

MAY 5TH. Admiral Arbuthnot having completed the repairs of his ships made the signal for sailing.

MAY 7TH. The rebels have used the ceremony of declaring the Convention Army prisoners of war and it is said have demanded Genl Burgoyne.

MAY 9TH. The rebel frigate Protector was brought in here —she mounts 26 guns.

MAY 10TH. Great riots have lately happened in Philadelphia about paper money, which it is said is entirely out of

[1] See note on p. 112.

circulation—as no person will take it. 1000 paper dollars are given for one silver.

MAY 12TH. The rebels are sending all the men they can possibly spare to the south'ard—Genls Wayne and LaFayette are both gone with different detachments.

MAY 17TH. Genls Phillips and Arnold have entered Virginia with 3000 men and have already defeated several bodies of militia, burnt a number of vessels and magazines and destroyed or took 7000 hogsheads of tobacco.

MAY 20TH. Genl Greene marched with his beaten army to Camden with intention of taking some of our exposed posts. Ld Rawdon who commanded in Camden marched out with about 800 troops on the 25th of last month and in a pitch'd engagement routed Mr Greene a 2nd time with the loss of 500 men.[1] Ld Rawdon had two hundred of his men kill'd and wounded. It is said Mr Greene is measuring back his steps with the utmost precipitation for fear Ld Cornwallis should cut off his retreat, and that his army deserts by hundreds.

MAY 21ST. Being determined on going home—as they will not employ any of the Northern Army here and the Admiral has refused us a convoy for Canada—went to Mr Tomkyn agent for transports who gave me an order for a Cork victualler; the Cork Fleet are ordered to sail the first of next month.

MAY 27TH. On the 23rd of this month received a letter from my Mother with the afflicting intelligence of the loss of

---

[1] Rawdon, left in command of the scanty defences of the Carolinas, checked Greene at Hobkirk's Hill—Hughes's report of Greene's flight was mere rumour. Rawdon became Earl of Moira and Marquis of Hastings, Governor-General of India.

my Father—the most indulgent and affectionate parent. He departed this life at Chambly on the 4th of Oct: 1780 being carried off by a violent fever. He was the humane soldier, a tender affectionate father and an open-hearted honest man; he was major of the 53rd Regiment and a veteran, having served His Majesty forty years.

MAY 28TH. Heard that my brother, Ensn John Hughes[1] of the 33rd Regt was wounded in the engagement at Guildford Court House. Am at present in such distressed circumstances that I have not cash sufficient to purchase myself a crape for my Father.

JUNE 3RD. Sir Henry Clinton ordered all the Canada officers to remain at York as there is a prospect of a convoy for Quebec.

JUNE 5TH. Ld Cornwallis has formed a junction with Arnold's detachment at Richmond, Virginia—Genl Phillips is dead, being carried off by a violent fever.

JUNE 9TH. Applied by memorial to the Commander in Chief to go to England, as my private affairs required my presence.

JUNE 10TH. Received orders to embark for Europe on board the frigate Confederate and take command of some invalids who are sent home to pass for Chelsea Hospital. Waited on Major Mackenzies, settled the invalids' accounts with their respective regiments and put all my men on board. At 11 a.m. made the signal for sailing and went down to Sandy Hook, about 30 miles from York—we shall remain here a few days as our convoy are not at present all ready for sea.

[1] Thomas Hughes's youngest brother. He served in America from 1781 to 1785.

JUNE 12TH. Am extremely pleased with my messmates, who are a genteel set of officers and make the ship as agreeable as they can to me. Landed at the light house, Sandy Hook, for the pleasure of a walk but it was so sandy and was so troubled with muskitoes that I was glad to be on board again.

JUNE 13TH. Admiral Arbuthnot with five sail of the line and two frigates anchored off the Hook—the Royal Oak one of his 74 gun ships was so leaky from being grounded on the chevaux de frise near the North Battery at York that she is sent to Halifax to be docked. Genl Arnold with a few troops arrived from Virginia; as they sailed past us could get no intelligence.

JUNE 14TH. Sail'd from Sandy Hook—cheered Admiral Arbuthnot in passing him, lay to outside the Hook to receive his final instructions and about 6 o'clock in the evening took the last view of America. Our convoy consists of the Cork Fleet of return victuallers and a number of private ships for London—in all above 70 sail. Our ships of force are the Confederate, 40 guns, Capt: Cummins (Commodore); Rainbow, 44 guns; Thames, 32 guns; Halifax, 20 guns; and two old Indiamen mounting 20 guns each.

JUNE 15TH. Chased some vessels which proved to be whale fishers from Canonicut; they were permitted to pass. A fine fair wind—am laid up with sea sickness.

JUNE 30TH. Spoke a vessel from Cork—no news. The wind continues at west and we shorten our voyage very fast.

JULY 2ND. Heavy gale of wind. Met a wreck but found no soul on board—all her masts were carried away.

JULY 4TH. A.m: the first foul wind we have had since our departure. P.m: the bad wind lasted 10 hours—it is again as fair as can blow.

JULY 11TH, 12TH, 13TH. Thick weather and very squally; obliged to lay to, though the wind is fair, as by our reckoning we are near Ireland.

JULY 14TH. Made Cape Clear—the finest weather imaginable; several boats came off and brought us fresh provision.

JULY 15TH. Sailed as far as the Old Head of Kinsale—when having received intelligence that the coast was clear from enemies' ships made the signal for parting with the victuallers. After laying to till we saw them off the Cove we made sail and stood over for Cape Cornwall. Our convoy is now reduced to thirty sail mostly merchant vessels bound to London.

JULY 16TH. A.m: a fine leading gale—all employed in mackerel fishing. 3 p.m: made the land of Cornwall and fell in with a fleet of coasting vessels under convoy of a 20 gun ship—in the evening saw the Scilly Isles. Our course is between them and the Cornish coast. Plentifully supplied with fish by the Cornish fishing boats—our want at present is of vegetables.

JULY 17TH. Pass'd the Lizard—being close in with the land and but little wind the country boats come off and supply us with every thing. Genl Howard of the Guards, who came in our fleet, received the Government dispatches from our ship and immediately landed to go post for London.

JULY 18TH. But little wind and that contrary. Put into Falmouth and being desirous of seeing the town was landed on the British shore after a 5 years' peregrination. Falmouth is pleasantly situated at the bottom of a commodious harbour. The town itself has no beauties being irregular; narrow dirty lanes instead of streets, and not a good house in it. It has two forts to defend the entrance of the harbour—Pendennis, which is strongly fortified and which when the additions now making are completed will be capable of standing a siege, and St Mawes Castle; this last is an old antiquated building of no strength, though they have lately raised a poor sort of battery mounting 12 cannon at the foot of it. Wrote to my friends.

JULY 19TH, 20TH. Having an uncle living near Falmouth, went to his house; as my coming to Europe was unexpected and my appearance greatly altered I was not known till I mentioned my name. Remain'd here two days and then returned to my ship with an intent of going again to my uncle's if the wind continued contrary. Just as I got on board the wind sprung up fair and we got under way.

JULY 21ST. A.m: saw a large fleet of 150 sail—spoke them —they proved to be a large supply for New York and the different ports in America.

P.m: spoke with the Courageux and Thunderer, 74 gun ships; they belong to the Grand Fleet consisting of 21 sail of the line all which we past off Plymouth.

JULY 22ND. Fell in with two fleets of coasters under convoy. As we were near the shore, our sailing was extremely agreeable from the numberless agreeable views; amongst them was a small encampment.

JULY. Having but light airs and those contrary we were all this month working up channel. As we kept close in shore most of the way we were plentifully supplied with provision and had always a changing landscape. On the 29th anchored off Deal in the Downs. We found five sail of the line just returned from the West Indies where they had been dismasted and were so much injured in other respects that they were obliged to be sent home to be refitted—this is part of the effects of the last hurricane which did such immense damage to the shipping and islands in those seas.

AUGUST 1ST. Having wrote the Secretary at War, received his orders for disembarking my invalids and for conveying them to London by any route I thought most convenient for the ease of the men. Put all the invalids on board a hoy and sent them up the river.

AUGT 2ND. Having settled all my ship affairs to my satisfaction went to Canterbury in the evening where I saw every thing curious in the cathedral, amongst others Thomas of Becket's tomb and shrine.

AUGT 3RD. Took place in the diligence; breakfasted at Rochester (having passed through Chatham) and in the evening reacht the metropolis. Being an entire stranger to the town, on my alighting at Charing Cross took a hack and drove to my Mother's at Grosvenor Place. Dismiss'd the coach at the corner of the street.

It is impossible to express my anxiety on my approaching the house, on account of the parlour windows being shut. I approacht the door and found Major Hughes on the plate. I knockt with eagerness, repeated it; no person answered and my heart died within me; knowing myself expected, what was I to imagine from a deserted house? every thing that was gloomy struck my imagination, the death of my mother, and the ruin of my friends. Notwithstanding the confusion I was in, my hand mechanically stuck to the knocker, till I was roused by a man who desired me to walk into his house, till the servant returned who had charge of the house, and who was gone a walking with the young gentleman. I was still afraid to ask for the rest of the family, but was agreeable relieved at hearing that Madam went into the country two days before my arrival. The man kept a publick house very near the house of my mother and on his leaving me in a room I took post at the window where I remained two hours, but no servant came. My anxiety returned, I thought the man had deceived me. I called him up, heard the same story, was satisfied for a little while; but in short a person must put himself in my situation to conceive what I felt when it came 10 o'clock; I was in the street every minute. At last I saw a person opening the door, and found it was the servant with my youngest brother. I found a letter from my brother-in-law Mr Stanhope, which cleared all doubts, and informed me that my Mother was paying him a visit, but that on my writing she would come directly to me. In a few days she came—and after a short stay in London I was prevailed on to go to Brighthelmstone[1] with Mr Stanhope to see my sister. Here I was first introduced to company, for, though a man of two and twenty, my long captivity and stay in America had quite rusticated me. Brighthelmstone is one of the first watering places in England, and was particularly brilliant this season, on account of the Duke and Dutchess of Cumberland being there, and there was likewise a report of the Prince of Wales's coming. All these inducements did not fail bringing belles and beaux from all quarters, and I found myself at once SEPT: launched into a sea of gaiety and dissipation; a thing impossible to be avoided, for all the amusements of the metropolis being here collected in a small vortex, it acts like a whirlpool, and permits no freewill to those who get within its influence; for my part I was out of my element. Being naturally of a reserved disposition, strongly affected by the mauvaise honte, owing to a natural bashfulness and want of

[1] I.e. Brighton.

good company, I could find little pleasure in a concourse of people whose only amusement was the exhibition of their sweet persons and a laborious attendance on the toilette. I however did my best and awkward enough to be sure, nor did I escape raillery from my frequent solitary morning walks on the side of the sea (which I frequently did in the most stormy weather, being very fond of viewing nature in her most tremendous appearances); a different reason was given, as men judge from their own feelings, and I was pronounced deeply in love with Miss Ann B—n, and I believe people persuaded the girl herself that it was so, as a relation of hers informed me afterwards that she had refused a doctor (an old man of 40) on my account. I give up the honour of the affair, though she was pretty, and will only say in my vindication that it was, on my part, only those civilities which I thought due to a person with whom I often danced, and who, as she was young and little known, was in greater want of the small attentions than those who had crowds of admirers at their feet. Had I been a person who would push himself forward in the world I might have done it here, as it was in my power to get into almost any line of acquaintance. People at these places, coming purely for amusement, are thrown together in a thousand different situations, where every one may make himself agreeable and little or no introduction is requisite; in fact these are the only places where the English unbend from their native formality and become sociable beings. These are the places for a man with a good face, and light pr of heels, to pick up a wife; it was even proved, whilst I was here, that the heels alone was the only requisite, as Mr R—e, both old and ugly, with a glass eye, carried off Miss W—l by dint of dancing; but I confess he danced in a very superior style. Brighthelmstone has little to recommend it, being surrounded by a common, and scarcely a tree to be seen; the bathing is pretty good. There are two Rooms; the new one is a very neat one. A theatre, raffling, the libraries, fruit shops, trinket shops, and the race ground constitute the principal amusements. We left Brighthelmstone and went to London in October and as my sister wished me to stay with her, I complied, and passed my time between Stanhope's house in Clarges Street and my Mother's. Stanhope though a man of family and expectancies had at this time greatly outrun himself, and was after a variety of shifts and escapes at last arrested, and after a stay at a spunging house removed to the King's Bench; nor did I come off scot free, for having kickt a bailiff and his employer down stairs, when on a visit to Stanhope (by which he made his escape), I was taken up, carried to the bar in Bow Street, bound in two sureties and at last obliged to pay 10 guineas to get clear. My sister being very ill from a fright and miscarriage and her husband in so disagreeable a situation, she was prevailed on to go to my Mother's, who was removed to Vauxhall Place. Time, and the treatment from our Mother, who is the best of parents, brought her to her former serenity, and at last she used to go frequently to Stanhope in prison, myself her constant escort, unless (as it sometimes happened) that my Mother took that office.

Being at this time in an ill state of health, from an inflammation in the stomach, I obtained leave by a physician's certificate to stay at home, and not to join my Regt in Canada. Vauxhall was almost my constant residence, a large garden belonging to the house found me exercise and amusement. In May I went to Bath, to look out a house for my Mother; but not meeting with one to please, soon returned. Whilst at Bath I passed my time very agreeably with Capt: B—w, who was there with his new married lady; on my return to town I found it was reported amongst my acquaintance, that I had gone on a matrimonial scheme, and that I was to be married to the sister of Capt: B—w. The summer passed, during which I scarcely visited Town. In December my eldest brother returned from America, a Capt: in the 7th Regt. As he was not pleased with our situation in the country, we removed the beginning of the year into Town, and had a house in London Street, Rathbone Place. During this time Mr Stanhope still remained in confinement and Mrs Stanhope, being reconciled to his situation, stayed more with him than her friends could wish, as her health visibly declined; she however acted the part of a good wife.

# 1783

Having a strong desire to learn French, and finding it impracticable to learn it properly at home, I took the resolution of going to France for that intent—and as I have never enjoyed my health since my return from America I wished to go to a place remarkable for good air, and after various reports fixed on Boulogne.

On the 9th of June I went on board the Calais packet, Capt: T. Meridon, which then lay at Blackwall—in the evening we made sail down the river. We had on board a French lady, an English miss going to a convent at Montreuil, and an old French gentleman who was going to Montpellier for the recovery of his health. We were accompanied to Gravesend by a party of young London cits by way of frolick; during the whole time of their stay on board they did nothing but eat, drink and smoke. About 12 o'clock we anchored at Gravesend and as it was a fine night I went on shore with the Londoners, who by this time had enough of their amusement and were considering how to get back in good time to attend their shops as for to-morrow. In getting into the boat after they were all seated, I unfortunately stept into some dirty water at the bottom and splasht the Sunday coats that were displayed around me, to the great terrour and dismay of the owners. On our getting to a tavern I took leave of my friends and went to bed, leaving them at liberty to clean their coats and say what they pleased on the disaster.

Monday morning after clearing out and receiving a visit from a Custom House officer who charged us 6 pence a head for the honour of his visit, we hoisted sail and, having but little wind, anchored at night off Margate but at too great a distance to land. My ladies disliking their beds chose to sit up all night. I was not galant enough to assist at their vigils and went to what was called a bed to quiet some qualms (not of conscience); sleep came to my relief and Tuesday was far advanced without my dreaming of it. It was weighing the anchor that awoke me; the tyde was just turned in our favour—as I was not undressed, to open my eyes and get on deck was the action of a minute. Breakfast was ready but as the captain did not think milk and soft bread any way necessary for folks at sea he took care not to be at the expense of providing it; as I hate tea without milk I attacked some brandy and water and which I believe preserved me from sea sickness. I observed we had lost one of our company, the old French gentleman; and I descended to the large cabin to ask after him. I could observe nothing but a large cur popping his nose out of a shut up berth; on my calling him, the Frenchman, who was behind in the berth, made his appearance and began a panegyrick on his dog—it was the most sensible, the most affectionate creature breathing, and had he but a sous the cur should have half, for a proof of his sensibility. He told the following story: some time since his wife fell ill, the dog would never leave the room for four weeks. She died; when the dog found that his mistress took no more notice of him, and that all his caresses received no return, as if sensible of the reason he left the chamber and would never enter it again, though his master enticed him with every thing he could think of for months after. At five in the evening we enter'd the harbour of Calais, in company with the Dover packet. The shore was lined with people dressed in their best clothes, as it was a Holy Day. Just as we came to the wharf, we saw a number of fellows pushing each other to get first; we were looking very coolly on them, when in an instant they jumpt into our ship and stunn'd us with their importunities. It was the waiters of the different inns come to request the honour of our company. We preferr'd Mons! Designe's and as soon as we had got the ladies on shore we followed a cringing rascall with his hat under his arm to the tavern. Designe's is one of the largest inns I ever saw and consists of several courts; it is almost a town of itself. The first thing we saw was a monstrous pair of jack boots not unlike a couple of portmantuas standing in the yard, and immediately after appeared Mons! le Cook with a monstrous bag wig. The ladies were inclined to mirth and they had such a number of incentives that I really feared they would have affronted the French beaux and belles by their hilarity. As there was no Comedy we traversed the town in the evening—it is on the whole a dismal place and nothing but the troops and passengers can keep it alive. I could not help thinking as I passed the rampart what a difference between the ancient and modern way of taking towns, when Calais could keep one of our most powerful kings a year before her gates. The first thing to be done on the 10th of June was getting the baggage on shore; the ladies beg'd my assistance as the Capt: did not seem inclined to trouble himself about them though put under his protection. As the ladies had a quantity of pins and needles which are seizeable I was obliged to blind the Custom House officer; which I did effectually with a three livre piece, for though he opened the box, and pulled out some thousands of pins &c, which were unfortunately at the top, he obligingly turned away his head whilst I put them in again. My return to the inn relieved the ladies from their pin fright. I found the Captain of the vessel with them, and as he was going to Boulogne he proposed hiring a coach for the whole; an assent being given in about 10 minutes we rattled through the streets drawn by six horses. We were stopped at the Barrière for passes, but the guard being informed that our names had been given in the day before, we were suffered to proceed. All strangers, on their arrival at the French frontier towns, must give in their names, and these are all sent to Paris. We dined at ⟨*blank*⟩ and arrived early in the afternoon at Boulogne; we put up at the Lion d'Or in the Basse Ville kept by an Irishman. Having a letter of recommendation to Mr B—n, I waited on him, and he understanding my plan of staying to learn French proposed my messing with some French officers in the Haute Ville, as the lower town was full of English. In a few days I got settled; I lodged in a house for 12 livres a month, and messed at a traiteur's for 42 livres per month, which provided me with breakfast, dinner and supper. My messmates were two old officers, an abbé, a lawyer, and a surveyor of the roads; we dined at 12 and supped at 8. At first I found myself awkward—their victuals, cookery, hours, all displeased me; in a month I became quite reconciled even to the toast and water drink of my companions, and drank little else during my stay in France. I now followed a regular mode of passing my time; I rose at six, walked till seven round the ramparts, then fenced, at 8 breakfasted; wrote French till eleven, when my master came and stayed till 12. Dinner was over before two when I took a short walk, and then at my French till five and had a holiday the rest of the evening. Having soon an acquaintance with the family of Mrs Nicolls I became soon so intimate, that I seldom passed an evening but at her house, or where her family was engaged, so that at last it was a thing of course to invite Mr Hughes with the Nicolls. The politeness I received and the obligations confer'd on me by this family broke through all my resolutions. In two months I was acquainted with every English family in the town, and I must remark the Boulogne mode of visiting. On a stranger's arrival, if he chooses to be acquainted, he goes round the town in the morning and drops cards wherever he pleases for the gentlemen; he repeats his visits in the evening for the ladies. This mode is adopted from the idea that families may come who wish to be retired; of course it is at their option to see company, or not, as is best suited their circumstances or inclinations. In August I forsook my mess and got into a French boarding house. My mornings I still preserved for study, but from 4 o'clock in the evening, till 12 at night, I was in English company, so that my evening undid my morning meditations. Often did I make resolutions of withdrawing myself from the English; and at last finding the Nicolls proposed leaving Boulogne in September I thought it would be ungrateful to leave them till their departure. Just about this period a large abscess was discovered in the side of Miss H. Nicolls, a pretty accomplished girl of thirteen; she had concealed the affair for three months lest it might make her mother uneasy. It was found out by its breaking in bed, and on its being opened discharged above a quart of matter. The sufferings of this child must have been beyond belief, but she was of an angelic disposition, and surpassed most grown people in quickness of comprehension and sensibility of heart. As she was of a delicate constitution the doctors pronounced her case very dangerous. No one can conceive the anguish of the fond indulgent parent, whilst the patient bore all with fortitude and smiled at torments. What a sight for me. I knew not whether to pity or admire most. My attendance was if possible more constant than ever; every evening we formed small parties to amuse at home, and in fine weather I used to escort the two other Miss Nicolls in their country rambles. Boulogne is divided in two towns, perfectly distinct from each other; the upper is situated on a hill almost entirely inhabited by French, and is surrounded by an old rampart, on which are the publick walks which are very pleasant; it is about three quarters of a mile in circumference, and has two churches and as many convents. The lower town is mostly inhabited by French and English traders, and is built on the flat by the harbour with one or two streets running up the hill to the upper town. The harbour which can only be entered at high water has a mole and small fort for its defence; small forts are scattered along the coast to prevent the landing of an enemy in those few places which are accessible. The sea shore and the cliffs over them afford pleasant rides and walks with a distant view of Dover Castle and the coast of England. Nor is the interior part of the country without its beauties—fruitful vales, barren hills, hamlets, castles, woods, all conspire to form a sweet variety; and I really think Boulogne and its environs equal in point of natural beauties to most places in England.

Here I led the life best suited to my inclination, and which I can look back on with pleasure; it was tranquillity without insipidity, cheerful, but not riotous. The morning was dedicated to study and the evening to amusement. The English at Boulogne were always in a state of warfare with each other, but we never interfered and were equally caressed by both parties.

The summer passed without bringing about the recovery of Miss Helen, who was so reduced in September that her removal was impossible, or at least the surgeon said so, and we all doubted her ever getting the better of her disorder.

[ 129 ]

In November they began to have balls once a fortnight in the lower town. The playhouse was changed into a ballroom by covering over the parterre, which gave us room to dance six sets of cotillions, which was the only dance; indeed once or twice the French out of politeness offered to dance an English country dance but they made such work that we never desired them to repeat it. I am not surprised the French prefer their dances to ours; they are much more pleasant and give more opportunity of showing good dancing. The French beaux, particularly the officers, dance with great agility and are fond of capers, which they perform equal to our stage dancers; not having so much mercury in my heels, I was obliged to go on in a more humble style. We paid thirty sous for admittance, and paid for what refreshments we called for; the balls began at five and were over by eleven.

## 1784

At Christmas, a set of young comedians came to town; they were all children, and performed extremely well. One girl had the finest voice I ever heard. Boulogne was not rich enough to support them, and in a month they left us. We had masked balls during Carnival twice a week, Thursdays and Sundays; the Sunday one was only six sous, and was calculated for servants &c. People of consequence used to go under cover of a mask, and see the amusements which, continuing most of the night, used to exhibit towards morning scenes of riot and debauchery. The common people have the same dances as their betters, and I have seen a parcel of fishermen's children, barefoot and with scarce a rag to cover them, dancing cotillions on the sands, much better than they are sometimes done in the Bath rooms.

In January a feu de joie was fired and Te Deum sung for the peace, which was finally settled between Britain, on one hand, and France, Spain, Holland, and America on the other, by which America was declared independent by Great Britain, who lost by the war her blood, her treasure, and an empire, owing to a cursed faction and weak ministers. My leave of absence being almost expired I began to be anxious about my return to London, and about the middle of February left Boulogne on a small vessel for London. I was accompanied by young Nicolls; the rest of the family were obliged to stay, on account of Miss Helen, who was in a most deplorable situation. To say I left Boulogne with regret is saying but little. The politeness and attention from the Nicolls family were engraven on my heart nor shall time ever efface the remembrance; if it should, be thou, Paper, the witness and monument of my ingratitude!

We had a short passage, and landed at Greenwich with some difficulty on account of a quantity of ice from the severity of the season. We neither saw or heard of any Custom House officers; an extraordinary circumstance for people who landed so near London, where we arrived about two o'clock in the afternoon. Nicolls would go to a house in the City where his friends had ordered him, and I revisited my Mother's; in a few days Nicolls returned, by Dover, to Boulogne. Finding that the time for joining my Regt was approaching very fast, and not over-desirous to go back to Canada where I had no prospect but of wasting a few years without profit or advantage, I attempted to exchange into an East India Regt, but as at this time the East India Regulations[1] were on the carpet from which some people (I do not know why) promised themselves great advantages, I could get no person to exchange unless I paid a difference which neither my purse nor inclination would permit me. I then wanted to go out a writer but ⟨as⟩ I had neither friends nor money of course that idea was chimerical. At this time there was no person at my Mother's but myself—Capt: Hughes was with his Regt, my youngest brother and sister at school, and my sister Eliza almost constantly with her husband in the King's Bench.

In March the family of Nicolls came to London; the death of Helen broke their tie to the Continent, and the recollection of their loss disgusted them with Boulogne. They stayed but a short time in London and went to Bristol, their place of

---

[1] A first *Regulating Act*, bringing the East India Company's settlements under the control of the Government, had been passed by North in 1773. Pitt's *India Bill* of this year (1784) revised this Act and strengthened the control.

residence. My friend Hamilton being in Town, agreeable to his annual custom, we were inseparable companions; a conformity of disposition that had made us chums at Eaton, cemented into friendship as we grew older, and being both idle men we were never so happy as when we were together. His horses &c. were always at my service, and Ranelagh was generally our resort twice a week. Nor shall Lady Jane be forgot who in our little soupées used to enliven the moderate glass, and give a zest to friendship; and I hope the time will come when Sir William, Lady Jane, and Sir Thomas will meet in the same disposition towards each other as at parting. Hamilton left London as usual in June, after repeated requests for me to go to see him at his father's near Exeter. The Nicolls wrote me also positively to go to them at Bristol, but I was soon roused from all my agreeable reveries by a thundering order from the War Office against all absent officers. Leave was now expired, and as I had received one of the circular letters from the agents, to say that my pay was stopped, and that my commission would be given away unless I joined my Regt, I was very anxious to go to Canada; and at last settled with Mr Houghton of our Regt to go with him in a packet that was just then ordered to sail for Quebec—I was however very near staying another year as, without my knowledge, Mrs Rolle had applied, to have my leave prolonged, to the Secretary at War; which being granted, I was much surprised, on waiting on him, to be told that I might stay till next spring. For this application of Mrs Rolle I was obliged to Miss B—, who thought it would oblige my family by keeping me at home, and therefore requested it as a favour. It was a pity that something of more advantage to me had not been asked, for the same interest would have procured me a company as easily as leave of absence. Being determined to go to Canada I withstood the solicitations of my friends, and after making an apology to Mrs Rolle for not accepting the leave that she had got for me, I left my Mother's on the 5th August with intention of leaving London immediately. I was however disappointed, for Houghton being ordered to carry out the dispatches to Genl Haldimand we were detained two days more; but as I hate taking leave, I never returned to my Mother's, but stayed at a Coffee House. We left London at one o'clock in the morning of the 7th and were in Exeter at 7 o'clock the morning after—I had no time to see my friend Hamilton as we only just took a breakfast. The roads being bad we did not arrive at Falmouth till 3 o'clock in the morning of the 9th and on the 10th sailed in the Speedy packet, Captain d'Auvergne; I had no opportunity of seeing my relations, without running the risk of my passage. Seven packets sailed from the harbour with a fair wind, which soon failing us, we were the next day off the French coast. On the 12th our companions separated for their different ports. There were but three passengers in our ship, Capt: Ennis, 29th, Houghton and myself; we paid forty guineas each, and lived as well as people on board a ship could. The Captain keeping a table fit for an alderman, gave all sorts of wines and had every convenience. The Speedy is one of the largest packets in the service, has two cabins which we called the drawing room and parlour, and were used as such, and she had small cabins for a dozen passengers—nothing but sea sickness prevented my passing my time agreeably. On the 31st of August we made the Banks of Newfoundland having seen but one vessel (a Frenchman) in our passage. Here we were obliged to lay

AUGT 7TH

[ 134 ]

to for two days in a gale of wind; but as we had fine clear weather and the ship rode like a cork on the waves and kept herself quite dry, there was nothing disagreeable in it but the delay; our amusement was finding out the highest billows which were of a tremendous heighth. A calm succeeded, and we caught plenty of fish. In a day or two we got amongst the fishing vessels and on the sixth September made the French islands of Miquelon and St Pierre; on the 7th we passed the Island of St Paul's in the Gulf of St Lawrence, on the 8th saw Anticosti, where we were beating off and on in the mouth of the St Lawrence for some days, and on one of our tacks saw l'Isle Percée. Thick heavy weather and a fair wind carried us to Bic in thirty hours; we anchored there and took in our pilot on the 14th. The three next days we made but little way being becalm'd off the mouth of the Saguenay River which disimbogues itself into the St Lawrence with such violence that you cannot pass it at the distance of two leagues without a stiff breeze. A fair wind on the 18th September blew so hard that our ship in spite of a rapid current brought us to Quebec (forty leagues) in twelve hours; we saw the settlements, villages, churches, &c in such a rapid succession that the country appeared much better settled than it really is. The first French settlers that we met in the St Lawrence are at St Barnabas two leagues below Bic, and about fifty from Quebec; however you cannot call the river settled till you get ten leagues higher, when the settlements begin to join, and you have a calash road the whole way. Most of the islands for this distance are settled, and have a pretty effect. The principal island is Orleans, about twenty miles long; it is well cultivated and has a number of good houses on it. It lies in the middle of the river and forms two channels, both of which open into the

Basin of Quebec, but the south side of the island is the passage
for ships; at the bottom of Orleans is the most difficult passage
in the river called the Traverse; the French made it more
difficult than it really is, that they might deter other nations
from the navigation of the river, and is now so well known
that there is no danger.

SEPT: 18TH. We landed about two o'clock, and went immediately to the Chateau. Houghton gave the dispatches, and
being introduced to the great man[1] we were all asked to dinner,
which was passed in that kind of constraint that one would
imagine a parcel of pigmies would be in, in the presence of
a giant that they feared would eat them, not a word above
a whisper, except from the general and those he choose to speak
to; as we were strangers, we were honoured with most of the
little conversation that was held. Our chief had a broken
foreign dialect and as he spoke French better than English it
was natural for him to prefer the former. The most agreeable
thing that I learnt at the Chateau was that our Regt, which had
been at Montreal for some time, was ordered to Quebec for
the winter and that I had no business to go any further;
Houghton went to Montreal on business and I got a house for
him and me, where I staid till the Regt came down the river
—about a fortnight, but I must do the justice to say that I was
treated by the officers of the garrison, which consisted of the
31st and 44th Regts, with the utmost civility, dining with some
one almost every day. Major Cotton was very polite, and
Capt: Parke gave me a general invitation. Our Regt relieved
the 31st who were ordered to St Johns and the Isle aux Noix.
Houghton soon returned, and being now one of the garrison,

---

[1] The Chateau at Quebec was the residence of the Governor, now Sir
Frederick Haldimand, a Swiss by birth. He was Governor 1778–84.

I got acquainted with a number of agreeable families; amongst others I was much indebted to Mrs Chandler, for numberless civilities. In November Genl Haldimand sailed for England, his leave for going home having come by Houghton. His departure flung the civil government into the hands of Lt Governor Hamilton, and the command of the troops devolved to Brig: Genl St Leger who made Montreal his head quarters and left Col: Hope to command at Quebec.

Nov:

Genl Haldimand embarked with all military honours as we lined the streets, and the shipping and garrison saluted him. To say what kind of a man Genl Haldimand was, would be too much presumption in me, as I had no knowledge of him but from report; he appears however to have made too much of his (what was called) friends and too little of the rest of the world. He was more feared than beloved, was arbitrary in his government. His foible was a fondness for engineering; but even his enemies allow him to have been a brave soldier. As the cold weather was now begun, and the ships all gone for the season, nothing was thought of but amusements. A small theatre was supported by means of a few theatrical officers, one or two of whom acted very well, and the house was very prettily fitted up. We had a publick subscription ball once a fortnight, private parties almost every night, which with carrioling in the morning made the time pass away imperceptibly.

## 1785

On the 18th January the Lieutenant gave a ball and supper to all that came passable drest in honour of the Queen's birthday, agreeable to the annual custom; it was a great mob, as it is expected that every person that is well, goes—and the French are too polite and love good things too well to make excuses on such an occasion.

The country was now so entirely covered with snow that you never knew whether you travelled over land or water; every thing was frozen but the main channel of the river. One of my principal excursions used to be to the falls of Montmorency, about 9 miles from Quebec in summer but not above six in winter as you cross the Basin on the ice. Genl Haldimand has built a pretty house just by the falls, the charge of which during his absence he gave Mr Chandler, and as Mr Chandler was fond of the place we had one or two parties a week to go and dine there. To see the falls in the highest perfection in winter, you must be on the ice at the bottom with the sun shining on them. The frost is so powerful that nothing is liquid but the perpendicular fall which is two hundred and forty feet. The ice forms a canopy over it, and leaves nothing at the bottom but a large cauldron big enough to receive the torrent; the sides are ornamented with huge icicles forming the appearance of a frozen cascade—with a few green firs rearing their heads out of the snow just to inform us that Mother Earth still lives below. With a lively imagination you might fancy a rock of crystal with a river gushing from a cavern at the top of it, the spray that rises higher than the fall freezing in the air looks like sparks of fire and forms in falling a pyramid at the bottom sixty or seventy feet high. Just at the top of the rock, where there is a projection, is built a small temple in the Chinese style; this is pushed so far forward that when in it you are absolutely over the fall and it requires a little resolution to look with tranquillity on the torrent below, for you do not see what supports you from within, and the temple is in a perpetual tremour. The river that forms the falls runs a good way up the country and exhibits, in summer, a variety of romantick scenes. The Canadian method of catching fish in winter deserves a remark. They build small houses of ice, large enough to contain three or four persons, in the middle of which they cut a hole to the water; at night, which is the time of fishing, they make a fire in the house which both attracts the fish and warms them, and they put down their lines through the hole. As there are generally a number of these huts on the Basin of Quebec all transparent it makes a very extraordinary and pleasing appearance on dark nights. The Canadians catch such quantities of a small fish called tom cods that they feed their cattle with them; the cows are very fond of this food however strange it appears. As I am on the marvellous topick I shall mention a received opinion on the effect of cold on frogs, toads &c: you find them in the winter froze quite like a lump of ice and so brittle that a fall on the ground breaks them to pieces; if you put them in cold water they thaw gradually and in a few hours come to life. I give this story from hearsay and do not vouch for it.

A person must have been in Canada a winter to feel the anxiety that every one is under at the approach of spring; as soon as the ground begins to show itself they begin to talk of the arrival of the ships, and wishing for impossibilities. We had some warm days even in March, but in April the sun was very powerful and made all travelling impossible, the streets up to your knees in water during the day and at night so slippy that you were always afraid of falling. On the 1st of May, the Basin still covered with ice, the town was agreeable surprised with the arrival of a ship from London; since our possession of Canada, no ship had ever arrived so early. The mountain brought forth a mouse; she had no news, and as she had pusht from England for the first market at Quebec, had brought no letters. We soon had other ships with letters from our friends, to hear of whose welfare is one of the first treats in the world. The town began again to wear an air of business, the river being soon full of ships, and the snow went away so fast that no winter was to be seen by the middle of May. By the first of June we were in the midst of summer—a scorching sun, dusty roads, and the woods full of muskitoes; such is the sudden transition from winter to summer in Canada that there's no spring, and it is a quarter that must be scratcht out of a Canada almanack. During the summer of 1785 I was a good deal at Sillery, the place Emily Montague[1] makes such a fuss about. The Revd Doct: Toosey lived there, and as his family were very polite, we had frequent parties at his house. The place itself so far from being a paradise is the vilest hole I was ever at; it shews the fertility of Doctor Brooke's fancy and I give him great credit not only for his picturesque landscape of Sillery but for his portrait of Bell Fermor, who is now transformed into a stiff gawky old woman, at least if as the world says he meant the character for Mrs A—p. Amongst

[1] *Emily Montague*, the first novel descriptive of Canadian conditions at this time, published in 1769, was written by Mrs Frances Brooke, wife of the Rev. John Brooke, Chaplain to the garrison of Quebec. Hughes apparently attributes the book to the Chaplain instead of to his wife. Arabella Fermor is a character in the story.

other excursions round Quebec, a party of us went across the
St Lawrence to the falls of Chaudière; it is a troublesome jaunt
as you have two or three miles of swampy wood to go through
before you can get at the falls. The River Chaudière is much
larger than Montmorency but the fall is not half so high;
there are advocates for both, as ⟨to⟩ which is the prettiest. For
my part I think the Chaudière the most romantick but if I was
only to see one of them, it should be Montmorency. As we
had lines with us, we caught a good dish of fish at the foot of
the falls. The Chaudière River falls into the St Lawrence about
7 miles above Quebec, opposite side and a little above Sillery.

The 22nd Regt left us at Quebec and went to Montreal in
June; in July the 65th Regt came from England or rather
Ireland and did duty with us at Quebec. The transports that
brought them carried away the eighth Regt. They had been
17 years in the country mostly in the upper posts, and were
rather a Regt of invalids than soldiers; as our Regt was very
weak we were obliged to take some drafts from them who were
no great credit to us, being the worst looking soldiers, and
drunkenest men that ever carried a musket. The 65th on the
contrary were all young men, great martinets, but so completely germanised both in dress and manœuvres that it was
some time before we could think them our brother soldiers.
We found them a genteel corps and were always on a friendly
footing with them.

Quebec the capital of Canada is about 450 miles from the
mouth of the River St Lawrence. It is built on a high point
at the head of a Basin about six miles wide and looks to great
advantage from a ship as she comes up. It is divided into upper
and lower town: the lower consists of a market place and one
or two streets which run along the shore and close to the hill

on which stands the upper town; this is mostly inhabited by merchants many of whom have good wharfs and large store houses. A street of steep ascent leads to the upper town where are the barracks, the Chateau, a market place, a parade and several convents; this is built on a flattish ground about half way up the hill and has a good rampart towards the country. On the summit of the hill called Cape Diamond is built the citadel, consisting of lines and forts for about six thousand men, but these works are far from being finished and I imagine never will as the frost destroys almost every year the works of the former. In some measure this has been remedied by making use of stone to fill up the works instead of earth, which is hard to be got, as there are not more than three or four inches earth that cover the rock on which these works are. Was an enemy to batter these works, the stone splinters would drive the troops away that defended them. Every person knows of the attack made on this place by the Americans under Arnold and Montgomery, which would certainly have succeeded had they marched into the town and not paraded so long on the Heights of Abraham. The inhabitants were divided and in great confusion, the gates of the town open and no military force capable of opposing them; the Americans hesitated—a few resolute people shut the gates, and the arrival of Sir Guy Carleton saved the town and province.

In November our civil governor Hamilton being recalled went home, and Hope, made a Brigadier by the selling out of General St Leger, had the entire command of the province as Commander in Chief and Lieut: Governor. The recall of Hamilton was much regretted by the province at large as he had made himself popular by his polite behaviour, and the passing of some laws which favor'd the people more than was judged consistent with the interest of Great Britain. Houghton of Ours having been long ill with the rheumatism obtained leave to go home in the same ship with Governor Hamilton— as he was pay master to our Regt, I undertook to act for him, agreeable to his request. At this time went home Joseph Brant[1] the Mohawk, much against the inclination of General Hope, but, as Brant was determined, Hope was obliged to comply. He went home in behalf of the Indian nations who had joined us during the Rebellion, but had been entirely forgot at the Peace and left to the mercy of the Americans. Brant, though born a savage, had received his education in New England where he learnt English pretty fluently—he wrote well, which with some little reading and a good natural understanding had rose him to be the first man of his nation. He was certainly the best person that could be employed by the Indians in such an embassy, as they were certain he would speak their sentiments, being himself so deeply concerned in the general misfortune.

[1] A Mohawk chief, of Iroquois descent. As a boy he attracted the attention of Sir William Johnson, Superintendent of Indian Affairs, who had married his sister and directed his education. Brant remained devoted to the British cause and in both the French and American wars led raids on the enemies of the British. After the war he settled with his people i Canada. He visited England in the winter of 1785–86.

The winter past like the former only that the main channel of the river was froze which permitted our passing to the Point Lévis side, and which is of great benefit to the Quebec markets. Early in May we were told to prepare ourselves to relieve the 31st Regt at St Johns and Isle aux Noix—but our route was changed soon after and on the 25 May we left Quebec in boats to go to Montreal; the morning of our departure Captains Wiseman and Scott joined us from England. On the 27th past Trois Rivières which is a straggling place of 3 or 400 houses and lay at Pointe du Lac where the first division of the 22nd Regt who we were relieving past us; on 28th crost Lake St Pierre and lay at Berthier opposite the mouth of the Sorel River; on the 30th arrived at Montreal. The whole way from Quebec to Montreal is settled on both sides the river, and the sailing up is more like a pleasure party than a voyage; but the most pleasing part was to observe the progress of the spring which at Montreal is at least three weeks earlier than at Quebec though the distance is only 130 miles. As we were informed that Montreal was only a resting place, we did not get so much acquainted with the townspeople as we might have done. It is a large town, the suburbs included not much less than two miles long. It has some old fortifications but being commanded by a hill can never be a place of strength; it is built on a plain and ships come up to the town, but the river is not navigable for vessels any farther and it is with great difficulty they come so far—nothing but a thunder storm can bring them to the wharf, as the current is like a mill stream. Ships are sometimes longer in coming the last two miles than they are in their voyage from England. The environs of

Montreal are extremely agreeable, especially the ride round the Mountain where you view the River St Lawrence with all its windings for forty or fifty miles—at Montreal it is about two miles wide, but a few miles above the town it is five or six. The hill itself is cultivated almost to the top and has a number of country houses and Canadian habitations on its sides.

JULY

JULY 24TH. The latter end of July we were ordered to the back posts[1] to relieve the 32nd Regiment. Our first division of five companies, one of which (the Major's) was under my charge, marched from Montreal to La Chine on the 24th July; as we knew every thing was dear at the posts we were going to, we carried a good stock of those things that we imagined necessary. La Chine is nine miles from Montreal and is the place people going to the lakes take boats, the river being too rapid from Montreal to go up with loaded bateaux. Major Mathews, our Commanding Officer, gave us a dinner in a polite manner and took his leave, as he was obliged to stay at headquarters for the arrival of General Carleton to whom he was aide de camp. Opposite La Chine is the Indian village of Caughnawaga. We loaded our boats this evening, in all sixteen. As we wanted some provision we did not go off so early from La Chine on the 25th as we expected; we went five leagues against a strong current, passed the first locks and lay in the wood above the mill locks. These locks, which were made by Capt: Twiss of the Engineers, are of great use; they admit two boats

JULY 25TH

[1] The series of trading posts on the St Lawrence and the Great Lakes, which were garrisoned for the maintenance of government and the protection of the fur trade in the West. They were eight in number— Oswegatchie, Oswego, Niagara, Fort Erie, Detroit, Michilimackinac and two at the outlet of Lake Champlain.

at a time and make those parts of the river easy navigation which were formerly portages where the boats were obliged to be unloaded and were got up empty with great danger. The north shore was pretty well settled, this day's jaunt.

JULY 26TH   26th July in our boats by daylight, two leagues to the rapids of the Cedars, boats unloaded, and baggage carried a mile and half while the boats were bringing up very slowly against the rapids, which roar and foam in a dreadful manner. As the Canadians settled here have plenty of carts, we were not long delayed, took boat again and went three leagues farther to the fort of Coteau du Lac, passed the locks with all the boats and lay all night in the Fort. At the rapids of Coteau du Lac[1] General Amherst lost many boats and the men were drowned; it could not be otherwise, the bed of the river being full of rocks over which the waters roll like waves in a stormy sea. In coming down boats must keep the south shore where there's a good channel; saw some bateaux go down with an astonishing rapidity, the Canadians singing and rowing all the time. Settled all the way today—the Canadian settlements end at the fort. On an island in the middle of the rapids is a second fort, where the Americans used to be confined during the war; many of them got away by floating down the rapids on pieces of timber, they must have been bold fellows and deserved their freedom. Leaving Coteau du Lac you have a disagreeable passage of a mile or two to get into Lake St Francois; if you miss your poling ten to one you go down the rapids in a part you must be lost. With Canadians there's no

---

[1] It was actually at the Cedars, immediately below Coteau du Lac, that Amherst, descending the river for the attack on Montreal in August 1760, lost 100 of his men.

danger, but our soldiers were very awkward and I was very glad when we got over it. Lake St François is about 8 leagues long and four or five wide; we got through it this day, in which we were lucky, as bateaux are often windbound several days at Coteau du Lac. Half way over the lake is a long point jutting out from the north shore on which is a small tavern as it is called, but where you can get nothing but a dram, and some milk; the people are English. We caught plenty of fish by trolling. Lay at Pointe du Lac; we are out of Canada and are in what is called its Dependencies.

JULY 27TH

JULY 28TH. As the American Loyalists[1] are settled here, I went with one or two more to breakfast with Capt: Duncan; as he was gone to lay out a new farm we were entertained by his wife, a very pretty girl of sixteen. We were politely received in an unfinished house of one floor and no other partitions than baize, which did not correspond with the tea equipage which was very elegant, everything that could being silver. As the lady had been accustomed to Montreal she seemed to regret the town life, though she said many genteel people were settled near her, and they did each other what civilities their situations would admit of. Went three leagues to Johnstown, as it is called; it has about 20 houses scattered amongst stumps of trees and half cleared lands, but every thing must have a beginning. The settlements join all along the north shore from Pointe du Lac. We were no sooner halted than a number of Highlanders came to us to ask the news

---

[1] Settlements of Loyalists were planted along the St Lawrence from Lake St Francis westwards as far as Detroit. The growth of these settlements and their desire for a representative government led to the division of Quebec in 1791 into the provinces of Upper and Lower Canada.

from below. They wore mostly something of the Scotch dress, either a bonnet, or kilt, and spoke such broad Scotch that I could have imagined myself in Scotland, had I not recollected that Johnson says there are no trees in the country. They all appeared contented, said they had good rich lands and expected a good harvest; they mentioned the great favors they had received from Government, which had not only provided them with their subsistence but had also furnished them with every article they wanted, even to thread and needles. I met an old man named Robertson, who was at the portage at Ticonderoga when I was made prisoner. He was so lucky as to make an escape; had he been taken he would have been hanged. I never heard what had become of him and was not a little surprised to see him. We went three leagues further and lay at the foot of the Long Sault, a very hard days work, the men sometimes up to the neck in water dragging the bateaux against a rapid current. As the river is here full of islands the channel we took is very narrow—well settled all the way.

JULY 29TH. Our first operation was to drag our bateaux up the Long Sault, which is a declivity of about half a mile over which the waters roll with astonishing noise and rapidity. As the river is here pretty wide, with some islands which form several channels, the view is grand, and would be a fine subject for the pencil. It is an immense cataract divided by islands covered with trees of the largest growth; some channels seem almost hid by the branches of the trees but wherever they leave small openings you see the stream foaming and dashing over rocks in every direction. The banks on each side are high and covered quite to the top with the finest timber. We had plenty of men and by putting 20 or 30 to a boat drag'd them all up by nine o'clock.

# *July* 1786

After passing the Long Sault the river opens and you have only a strong current till you come to Rapide Plat— six leagues. We got up the first part of the rapid and lay in a small bay. Some of our boats were left behind and mine amongst the rest; for the convenience of an awning I was with the Commanding Officer, and was obliged to lay on the ground for want of my baggage. The north shore well settled all the way; some of our gentlemen who walked for pleasure said they found a good path and that all the farms were very flourishing. We met Captain Duncan here with whose wife we breakfasted at Pointe du Lac.

JULY 30TH. Our boats all joined before sun rise. We got over the other part of the rapid and went three leagues to the Galops, which is a very difficult rapid, but as it is the last, the men work'd cheerfully. A little above the Galops on an island stand the ruins of Fort William Augustus. We went about three leagues and lay on a point opposite the fort of Oswegatchie where we have a few men; vessels used formerly to come down as low as this. We are now in the lake of a Thousand Islands which is three or four miles wide at this place; we are now at the end of the settlements —or at least only have a few scattered houses—till you come to Cataraqui 70 miles off where the Loyalists are again settled.

JULY 31ST. Rowed twelve leagues up the lake and lay on one of the innumerable islands with which this lake is almost covered. The one we encamped on, like most of the others, was only a rock with trees growing out of the clefts; we caught plenty of fish. Just before we landed we were caught with a thunderstorm, which dispersed the boats, as they all made to the first place of shelter, but we were all got together by sundown. Our island is about a quarter of a mile round, and I believe never was so well inhabited.

AUGUST 1ST. The lake so covered with islands that it is impossible to go without a pilot; the trees almost join over some passages and form a fine shade. We rowed thirteen leagues, halting about an hour to dine and rest the men. About six o'clock reached Carleton Island. We did not see the fort till we were close upon it; and notwithstanding what I had heard, it appeared to me an enchantment, when on turning a point of land—the first thing that presented itself was a vessel of two hundred ton and a boundless expanse of water that look'd like the sea—the fort which overlooks the water and stands on a rocky eminence—with the dock yard—and merchants' houses below; all together was such a contrast with what we had been going through, that I stared with astonishment and could scarcely believe myself so distant from the sea. Captain Ennis of 29th Regt, with whom I came from England, commanded at the post &c—we supped with him.

AUGT 2ND. The fort is nothing extraordinary; the ditch is cut out of the rock, but quite unfinished, some places not four feet deep; the bastions are the smallest things I ever saw; there are plenty of bombproofs, but all out of repair. Having seen all that was to be seen, and put all our things on board the Seneca, we embarked about one o'clock and sailed soon after. Passed the Duck Island and lost sight of land.

AUGT 3RD. Terrible sick, a large swell; in the evening got sight of the high land of Toronto; a foul wind.

AUGT 4TH. Off Niagara, but the wind directly out of the river; tacking all day.

AUGT 5TH. With great good luck just made the mouth of

Niagara River but it was late before we got over the bar. We were thirty hours within sight of the fort and were much afraid we should have been drove back, a very common thing; vessels are sometimes drove even from the bar and obliged to return to Fort Carleton, there being no port or anchorage between, but on the other hand it is an open lake free of shoals. In 1781 the ship Ontario was lost and nothing but a hat and drum case ever seen. It is imagined she overset, as the night after she sailed was very squally—84 men were lost. The distance from Carleton Island to Niagara is about 140 miles.

Augt 6th. Niagara stands on a point of land formed by Lake Ontario and the river that discharges itself out of the upper lakes. The fort towards the landing is stoccaded, it being in no danger from the water; on the land side, it has a regular hornwork, dry ditch and ravelin, with stone block houses in the bastions. The few houses that constitute the town lay in the low ground towards the river and are chiefly inhabited by merchants. On the other side the river, which is about 700 yards wide, the new settlements commence and extend a long way round Lake Ontario and up Niagara River to Fort Erie almost forty miles. The wind being favourable, instead of unloading at Niagara, which is the usual way, the ship went up to a place called the Landing, seven miles farther; for my part having breakfasted with Mr Kirkman of the 29th I chose to walk with one or two other lads of the Regt. The place called the Landing and where we found the ship is just at the foot of the rapids from the falls, and a boat cannot go 100 yards beyond the wharf. It is a romantick place and as the banks are extremely high they have a contrivance to drag goods up with a windlass and large machine that goes on skids. The river is about 200 yards wide, of great depth and very rapid—began to unload and draw up the baggage.

AUGT 7TH. Good part of the baggage being landed, we went through the operation of weighing and loading it on waggons. The portage of Niagara is farmed by a Mrs Stedman who charges four shillings per cwt for carrying it eight miles; Government allows so much to every officer, all above he pays for himself. Formerly there were no restrictions but such abuse was made of this privilege that it was obliged to be put a stop to. As there were not corps sufficient for the whole I was sent forward with three companies about 2 o'clock— with orders to make the best of my way to Fort Erie. At leaving the landing we marched up a high hill that gave a fine view of the country we had gone through, and of Lake Ontario, which really looked like the sea; in our march we were shewn the places that various actions had happened, between English, French and Indians. The road leaves the river at the landing and you see no more of it till you arrive at Fort Schlosser, eight miles from the landing and two above the falls; it is here more than a mile wide. The fort is a miserable place, no defence but a few pickets; Stedman's house to which we went is large, with a good orchard and fine farm yard. The waggons were not arrived and we took the opportunity of going to the falls; it was almost dark when we arrived and could not see it to perfection. It was the most magnificent scene that I ever viewed: the fall takes a curve like a bow across the river, and taking in the bend almost half a mile wide, 140 feet high, and perpendicular. The gloom and still-ness of the evening, the deaf'ning roar of the waters and the shaking of the ground gave an awful solemnity, and it is not easy to express what I felt and was sorry that the necessity of my speedy return to the party made me hurry back after a five minutes stay. The fall is divided by an island, on which, notwithstanding the great risk, people often go; Stedman has even made a potato garden there—and says there is no danger if you have men that understand poling and know the ground. The most extraordinary story is the effect the fall has on wild fowl such as geese, ducks &c, if they get into the strength of the stream, the velocity of the current prevents their rising and they go down and are dashed to pieces. Some people who have gone to the foot of the fall say there is a passage between the water and the rock, but the thickness of the air and the dreadful noise prevent going more than a few yards. The wood was so thick and it grew so dark before we got back that our guide trod on a snake, but it was luckily not a rattle-snake with which this part of the country abounds. We supt and lay at Stedman's.

AUGT 8TH. Having collected boats and loaded them, we left Fort Schlosser about eight o'clock in the morning, accompanied by some Indian chiefs who beg'd me to give them a passage. We rowed three leagues, after which the stream was too strong and we were obliged to pole three leagues more to Fort Erie; the last part of our voyage was very tedious on account of the great depth of water. The shore on the north side was pretty well settled as were some islands, the river of a great breadth and multitudes of fish, many of which we caught by trolling. Fort Erie is a stoccade now almost in ruins, situated at the entrance into Lake Erie. Two large brigs were at anchor off the Fort waiting for us—we put the baggage on board and sent off the boats for the other division, but it was nine at night before they could leave the place, and as I heard much about boats going over the falls by missing the channel I was very uneasy least some accident should happen. Lt Roche of the 34th commanded at the port, and as this was one of our reliefs he went to Niagara to settle some affairs previous to his departure.

AUGT 9TH. In the afternoon our second division, that we had left at the landing, arrived, and eased me of my fears, as our boats got down well. We all embarked and are ready for sailing, but the wind is contrary.

AUGT 10TH. Remained off Fort Erie. It rained most of the day and none of us had any desire to go on shore. The Fort is pleasantly situated and has a full view of the lake, which opens gradually about half a mile below the fort. There's a strong rapid which indeed may be look'd on ⟨as⟩ the head of the river that joins the two lakes—ships are sometimes forced from their anchorage opposite the fort and obliged to go down the rapids for shelter, but it requires a storm to bring them up again. The fort is stoccaded, but in a miserable situation, most of the pickets decay'd and many quite down. We were visited by some Indians who sold us fish for rum; they gave us a pike of 15 pounds for a pint and a piece of bread.

AUGT 11TH. Still at anchor; a fine day, most of us went on shore to walk, or go into the water. At 12 o'clock several Indian chiefs came to request our Commanding Officer's permission to go to Detroit in our vessels—they said they were going to a great council and were afraid of being too late. Though attended with great inconvenience to ourselves their request was granted. Forty of them were put on board the Dunmore; it is my good luck to be in the Rebecca.

AUGT 12TH. Sailed in the afternoon, but the wind fail'd us in the evening off Point Abino only 10 miles from the fort.

AUGT 13TH. Calm, and for my part terribly sick. We were three days on Lake Erie and did not arrive at the islands at the

head of the lake till the 15th. These islands go quite across the
lake and form several channels, but they are not
AUGT 14TH all navigable. The 15th left the islands and had
an open sea to the mouth of the river—about 40 miles;
we here overtook the Dunmore, who had
AUGT 15TH separated company some days before as she sail'd
better. The 16th we enter'd the river, which though 4 or
5 miles wide has only a very narrow channel for ships; both
sides of the river are settled, and many of the islands, with
which the river is thickly covered, are inhabited; as you go up
the river the settlements thicken and for some
AUGT 16TH miles before you arrive at Detroit it is almost
a continued village. Detroit is six leagues from the mouth,
and owing to little wind and strong current it was past three
o'clock p.m. before we got to the wharf. Our voyage was by
no means tedious; it was a most lovely day and all our musick
and drums were employed to announce our arrival—and which
really was the case as the 34th, whom we relieved, knew
nothing of our coming till the noise of our drums made them
suspect the truth. As it was too late to get matters arranged
we were ordered to disembark in the morning. Our journey
from Montreal to Detroit took us twenty two days, and we
were told was the most expeditious for a number of men that
ever was known. The whole distance is about 700 miles; from
Fort Erie to Detroit is more than 100 leagues.

AUGT 17TH. Disembarked and took possession of Fort
Lernault where we were order'd to remain till the 34th sail'd.
We now found that Major Ancrum of the 34th Regt was to
be left behind to command the garrison, a piece of intelligence
by no means agreeable to us and a great injustice to our
Commanding Officer who was almost as old an officer but

unfortunately for him no Scotchman. We this day dined with our new Commanding Officer and from some little misunderstanding between the Commandant of the Garrison and the Commanding Officer of our Regt plainly perceived there would be no great cordiality in future. The Regiment we relieved did not give us any reason to speak in their praise as every little thing that could be of service to us and which generally go with the post, such as the mess garden &c, was given away to some Detroit people, that is with regard to this year's produce; and the great affront from us that occasioned all this was our refusing to buy their horses, carrioles, and

AUGT 22ND calashes for which we had not the least occasion. They left us the 22nd and we made ourselves as comfortable as we could, but the people of the settlement were a little surprised that we did not follow the plan of the Regiment before us, and keep horses, give balls and races, and gamble. Our reply was that we were not men of fortune and that we intended living in such a manner that we could pay our debts when we went away.

Detroit is a small town of about 200 houses, fortified with an old stoccade and block houses, sufficient defence against Indians; at 200 yards further from the river on a small rise stands Fort Lernault which is a field work—square, with half bastions. The pickets of the town run up and join this fort which is in a very unfinished state and badly constructed; it only contains barracks for 140 men and would require 400 to defend it. The troops are quarter'd in this fort and in what is called the Citadelle which is a small part of the town picketed off by itself. The only publick buildings are the church for the Catholicks, the Council House, which serves as church and ballroom to the Protestants, and the Government House for the Commanding Officer; this last is an elegant house built in a modern style with a large garden that runs down to the river.

AUGUST. As we have the post of Michilimackinac[1] to garrison, Lt Houghton was detached with 40 men to relieve the troops at present there. The distance from hence to Mackinac is 350 miles, so that our cantonments take up 700 miles. To go to Mackinac you first cross Lake St Clair which is only 3 leagues above Detroit—it is 12 leagues over; you then go up the river St Clair 12 leagues more which carries you into Lake Huron. This lake is twice as large as Lake Erie; Mackinac is situated on an island between Lakes Huron and Michigan, which are joined by a small straight of five or six leagues wide. This is the last post for troops, but traders go from Mackinac up the Sault of St Mary's into Lake Superior, supposed to be the largest in the world. At the head of this lake they take to their canoes and go some hundreds of miles up rivers in different directions but mostly to the north west where they get the best furs; they often go so far as to meet the traders from Hudson's Bay, and some stay out eighteen months—from this last place of departure, at the head of Lake Superior, called Le Grand Portage. The way that we took is not the only way to go to the upper countries; there is another, shorter and which the traders prefer. The river St Lawrence near Montreal forms two branches; the one goes through the Lakes and was our route, the other runs more northerly and can only be navigated by canoes. This branch the trader mounts and has innumerable obstacles in his way, rapids, shoals, and portages every league. In seventeen or eighteen days they get up to the last portage—at this place

---

[1] This island post at the northern end of Lake Michigan controlled the entrances to the three lakes, Huron, Michigan and Superior.

they leave the river and cross the woods to the head of a small stream that empties itself into Lake Huron; this last carrying place is 7 miles. At the Sault de Ste Marie the two routes meet; from the small distance between the two water communications at the bottom of Lake Huron, the Indians have given the name of the Island to that immense tract of country that lies between them.

OCTOBER. In October we were alarmed by an inroad of the Americans into the Indians' country that lies between Fort Pitt and Detroit; they destroyed some towns belonging to the Shawnees' nation, took some prisoners and return'd. As our commandant was jealous of their intentions, and it was not known where they might stop, we were immediately put to work at Fort Lernault, which in its then situation was not defensible; a few days after we had commenced, an engineer arrived with orders from Genl Hope to put the fort in a state of defence, and our business became serious, some works that were to be executed at Niagara obliging Lt Humfrys (the engineer) to return.

NOVEMBER 6TH. Major Ancrum appointed me to act as engineer at a dollar per diem, which was confirmed by the general. My time was now pretty well taken up, and as the Commanding Officer of our Regiment had made me acting chaplain to the corps my income was greatly increased. I did my duty as Lieutenant in the 53rd, to which I acted as paymaster and chaplain, and every instant of spare time was taken up by my engineership. We worked hard at the fort, and though we had a severe frost most of November we made shift to put Fort Lernault in a state of security before the 10th December when it was impossible to work any more out of doors.

# 1787

During the winter we had a ball once a week, which with carrioling and parties of all kinds made time go away faster than we had imagined—in fact a Detroit winter is in all respects like a 1787 Canadian one except that its duration is not so long. The inhabitants of Detroit are a motley set of English and French and live much beyond their means—when we came the whole town was in a state of bankruptcy owing to a bad sale of furs last year—but though the *merchants* (as they all call themselves) could not pay their debts, they gave entertainments, and any person would have imagined from the extravagance and profusion that reigned in all the houses that trade was in the most flourishing situation. In March some bateaux arrived from Canada, which was the signal for the sailing of the vessels, so we were certain of the Lakes being open. In April orders arrived for Major Ancrum's joining his Regiment and giving the command of the port to Captain Wiseman, and he left us in May. In justice to this gentleman let me say that, though sometimes hurried away by the violence of his temper which made him do things not perfectly agreeable to those under him, yet he was a man of great generosity and could do favours in a way that added to the obligation; to me he was extremely attentive, and was never more pleased than when I went to his house without ceremony. His wife is one of the best of women and his daughters only wanted a little of the world to make them very agreeable companions. Ancrum in general was not liked, and was only regretted by those who were intimate with him.

MAY 24TH

JUNE 9TH. Wiseman had scarcely taken the command and got settled in the Government House, when the part of our

Regiment stationed at Niagara arrived to reinforce the garrison, under the command of Major Mathews—who also came to regulate a number of abuses that had insensibly crept into the government of the settlement. Before his arrival Wiseman had given me an apartment in the great house, and his coming made no change; we all three lived together. During most of the summer I was employed in laying an abattis round Fort Lernault, which was a work of time, being obliged to bring the trees near four miles and had only four horses in employ; other works went on at the same time such as repairing barracks, building ovens &c. In September I accompanied the major in an excursion down Lake Erie to lay out some towns and lands on the east shore; we were a little unlucky in the weather and want of provisions, which obliged us to return without finishing our business. In October we

OCTOBER went again and laid out about 20 miles in lots, which were on our return given out to different Loyalists. The most remarkable thing we saw was the remains of an old Indian fort, which it seems was built, before we settled the country, by the Indians in their own wars—and we saw a wolf and stag, the last of which took to the water and we chased two miles into the Lake and there killed him. Every evening during this party we were amused by the wolves who visited us, but we lost nothing. Had we gone for pleasure we might have killed great quantities of ducks and partridges; the major hastened our return as he wanted to go down to Canada and the season was far advanced. The Americans during the course of the summer had made great preparations to attack the Indians but it ended in nothing. In October Captains Wiseman and Baird were sent to an assembly of Indians with the yearly presents—the Indians amounted to three thousand and were supposed to be the greatest number ever collected on such an occasion. Joseph Brant with his Mohawks were among them, and at a congress held immediately after the distribution of the presents the Indians determined to go to war with the Americans, who had made great encroachments on their hunting grounds.[1]

NOVEMBER 4TH. On the 5th November Major Mathews left Detroit, universally regretted, and with great justice, as he had been indefatigable in his endeavours to assist the settlement. My appointment of engineer ceased the day he went away, the Major having been so good as to prolong my office as long as possible—indeed this is but a small part of my obligations to him. Wiseman reassumed the command; a few days after, Capt: Houghton arrived, to whom I deliver'd over the paymastership, and retired to my Lieutenancy, if I may be permitted to use the expression.

[1] The Indians were at war with the Americans down to 1794, claiming as their hunting grounds the lands north of the Ohio. They were angry with the English for sacrificing their interests in the Treaty of 1783, while the Americans on their side suspected the English of instigating the Indians to hostilities.

# 1788

Our winter did not begin till 6th Jan: 1788 but it came in with such cold weather that it frightened us; notwithstanding which the amusements of the carnival occupied the whole place, and in my life I never saw such feasting and drinking, dinner, suppers and balls every night; and at a dinner given by Wiseman on the Queen's birthday to 38 people they drank him a hundred bottles of madeira besides porter and rum. I only mention this to shew what the Detroiters are—for they drank the same every where. Their eating was in the same extravagant style; forty, fifty dishes were common, and the expense enormous—madeira sixteen shillings and porter eight shillings pr bottle, beef a shilling, veal and mutton eighteen pence per pounds, and so in proportion. My health had been long on the decline and this life, though I refrained as much as possible, almost knockt me up. On the fourth February the cold was so intense that madeira froze in a stove room where some of our people were drinking—the coldest day ever known at Detroit, the thermometer at fifty five degrees below freezing. One of the most favorite amusements was the country carriole party, which generally came three times a week during the season, and deserves mentioning. At the commencement of the season a paper goes round with the names of those who ⟨they⟩ imagine will subscribe and includes the generality of the town; those who wish their names to stay make a particular signature, and immediately two managers are appointed to regulate the party. These managers write down a very good dinner calculated for the number of subscribers, and then send a small note to each house telling the person what he is to

**FEBRUARY 4TH**

bring in his carriole—the families generally bring the meat part and the single men the wine and porter. Each gentleman likewise carries two plates with knifes and forks and two glasses. They generally go two or three leagues to some farm house, and about twelve o'clock have sufficient to make a country dance; the dancing lasts till three—then dinner comes in and at five they all go to their carrioles with the musick at their head—and so proceed in great order to the Fort. They seldom have less than forty or fifty persons, generally about thirty carrioles, and as they have rules to prevent passing each other on the ice, it has a very pretty effect. My health prevented my going to any more than one of these parties, but it was the most agreeable thing of the kind I was ever at—as there's no more ceremony than what is necessary to restrain rudeness.

Our winter express left us 20th February, having been stopt some time for the letters from Mackinac; on the 17th three Indians came from Mackinac in sixteen days. I wrote to my Mother and Major Mathews, and requested of the last leave to go to England in case our Regt was not relieved this year. The only news from our port was a circular letter from the Indians requesting the warriors of all the Canada nations to meet at a grand congress near Detroit early in the spring. It was pretty positive that the Americans were making preparations for entering the Indian territory, being provoked thereto by the scalping parties that some young savages had gone upon immediately after the congress last fall—against the will of the old men, who had attempted to settle the matter with the Americans, and sent some strings of wampum to lay the blame on their young men's rashness. No notice having been taken of their message, they beg'd the warriors to assemble, that they might not be caught unawares. The Indians had

been labouring under a dreadful plague to them: the small pox
—sent out amongst them from Fort Pitt, by the Americans
on purpose—or at least it was said so. More Indians died of
it than were destroyed all last war; and it was with the utmost
difficulty that it was kept out of the settlement of Detroit,
where it had never been. The 20th February I went in a
carriole to the mouth of the river to settle some disputes about
lands. The 21st went down the Lake which was quite froze—
indeed so much so that when we wanted to give the horse
some water we could not cut through the ice which was several
feet thick. I visited some of the settlers who had gone upon
the lots laid out by the Major and myself, and was pleased to
find them already so comfortable; they offered me butter for
sale but asked more for it than was given in Detroit. The
22nd I returned to Detroit, having made a very pleasant
excursion of about forty miles and lived on milk and eggs.

MARCH 18TH. In the beginning of March the weather
began to alter, and in a few days the river which had been long
froze broke up. On the 18th our express returned from
Niagara, having been eleven days on his return. With him
came a Colonel Conolly and son; they brought accounts of
a rupture likely to take place betwixt England and France[1]—
an unpleasant intelligence, as it will perhaps detain us in these
posts, from whence we expected to be relieved the ensuing
summer. Colonel Conolly came in some public employ—
supposed in the Indian line. Finding that my affairs on settling
with Captain Houghton would permit me to purchase the

[1] In 1787 England and Prussia intervened in Holland to restore the
Stadtholder who had been driven out. There was risk of war with France,
but her domestic situation prevented her from supporting the Dutch
Republican party.

Captain Lieutenancy, I wrote to the agents in the beginning of April by the way of Fort Pitt—the letter went by a

APRIL 7TH Mr Vincent, who came with Colonel Conolly and the Colonel employed in forwarding some connections which he wished to form with the Americans in the back countries. About this time I again began to act as engineer, being ordered to inspect a quantity of pickets which the Settlement of Detroit were ordered to bring in to

MAY repicket the town. On the 1st of May the first ship sailed for Fort Erie and about the middle of the month the vessels for Mackinac left Detroit—the ice always stays longer in Lake Huron than it does on Lake Erie, which makes the communication to open later and cannot be depended on for more than four months in the year. The latter end of May I accompanied the Commanding Officer in an excursion to our new settlement. We found several lots in a good state of improvement and the inhabitants much pleased with the land, which was mostly a fine rich soil. We were out five days owing to boisterous weather; the Lake was too rough for our boat and we were twice obliged to run ashore to prevent filling. We saw a good many flocks of wild pigeons, but their season was almost over—they had been so plenty that they were knockt down with sticks. I have myself seen a flock of many thousands, and the agitation of the air with their wings makes a noise like a strong breeze of wind. In coming home we stopt at a small island called Fighting Island, and seeing a woodcock, I immediately went in search of him; the grass was pretty high, and finding a good many birds was flattering myself with good sport. The second that I killed flutter'd a little way, and I called some men to look for it— but we were all glad to get away as fast as possible, as we found ourselves in a bed of snakes; they were in every direction and the ground so full of their holes that you could not step without covering some. A black snake caught one man by the shoe— and the only one we thought proper to kill proved a rattle- snake. We afterwards heard that no person ever went on the island to shoot, though there was plenty of game, on account of the snakes; some Indians however live there, and I saw some squaws working in a field who did not seem to mind

JUNE them. On the first of June a vessel arrived from Fort Erie and brought us the agreeable intelligence of our being to be relieved as soon as the troops could leave Canada, and that all ideas of a war with France were over. By the same packet the Commanding Officer was allowed a private clerk at 2/6 per day—this post was given me by Wiseman, who has always given me every mark of his regard to my family.

The Indians, having taken up the hatchet against the Americans, took a number of prisoners on the Ohio—most of whom they burnt as a sacrifice to the manes of their friends who were killed at the Shawnees' towns in the fall of 1786; some prisoners were however lucky enough to be brought to Detroit, and by the interest of Captain McKee with the savages restored to their liberty, amongst the rest a Mr Ridout. He was a merchant—had been collecting debts in the back countries and was going on his way to New Orleans, with what he had been able to scrape together. In going down the Ohio they were surprised at seeing a large boat near the shore, where they knew there could be no inhabitants. When they came near about forty Indians jumpt into her, and made after them; resistance being hopeless they surrendered—every thing was in an instant plundered, and Mr Ridout and his crew stript. When they landed they found the savage party consisted of 90 warriors of different nations; they had taken a boat the day before and had in all ten prisoners. The pipe was given to Mr Ridout to smoke, the savages shook hands with him and told him not to be afraid, and gave him some of his own chocolate on which they breakfasted. The next day the plunder &c was to be divided—each nation separated, and made their own fire—an old Indian gave to each party its portion of the booty, and all appeared contented. They then came to the prisoners. The first was given to a Cherokee who took him a little on one side and tomahawked him—the 2nd and 3rd as soon as taken out had belts of black wampum put round their necks and were carried away—the fourth was given to four young Cherokees who put him in the middle of them, and shook rattles made of deers' sinews round him, and then turning to the woods seemed to make some incantations. This made the prisoner very uneasy; he was a Mr Richardson, who it was imagined had been guilty of some crimes and was running from justice. Mr Ridout's turn was next. He was given to an old Shawnee who received him kindly; but at night he was tied by the arms and neck, and the rope fastened to a stake with a bell on the top of it, and at the same time they closed his fists and put on two leather bags over them. The party to whom he belonged intended to get drunk, and they gave him in charge to some Cherokees for the night—as he was in great pain from being tied so tight it was impossible for him to sleep though he had been inclined. He was laying before a fire and his guard opposite him when about at midnight he heard a drunken Indian giving the war hoop and soon after saw him coming towards him; he was painted black, had the tomahawk in one hand and scalping knife in the other, every thing that was furious was painted in his countenance. The tomahawk was lifted up, and one step more brought him within reach of Mr Ridout. That instant a young Cherokee awoke, jumpt across the fire, and caught the arm of the savage, who after a struggle was obliged to go away. He returned a second time when he thought them asleep, but being again disappointed, he grew outrageous and the sober Indians seeing his situations tied him neck and heels and laid him along side them. This is but one of numberless escapes that Mr Ridout experienced in a stay of three months. He was equally lucky at arriving at the Indian village to which his party belonged. It is the custom when they bring home a prisoner for the women to turn out and flog them, and they often do it so effectually that they die under the operation. The old Indian, his master, stopt short at a quarter of a mile from the village and painted him red, telling him not to be afraid for that if he intended to do him any harm he would have painted him black. Most of the women of the village were in the fields at work and he only got one blow from an old woman who flung a log at him. During his stay at the village, a prisoner, that was brought in after him, was burnt, and the execution was so near the hut Mr Ridout staid at, that he heard the cries of the unfortunate victim. They tormented him two hours, and some Indians who belonged to his hut came and boasted of the variety of torments that they had made him suffer. This gentleman staid three months in this situation and at last was brought in on his promising to pay £100 that his master owed to a person at Detroit.

JUNE 26TH. Five companies of the 65th Regt arrived to relieve our Regt; the next day a company was sent off to relieve the post of Michilimackinac, and the day after six companies of our Regt embarked and fell down the river a few miles. We were obliged to leave two companies behind as we had but two vessels—in one of which I was put to command, with five companies, and the other, which was a small sloop, carried Capt: Wiseman and his company. We were very much crowded and, to make the cabin more comfortable, I had the company of three married ladies of our Regiment, who would not visit or speak to each other. My first care was to attempt a reconciliation, which I effected in some measure, or at least they kept up some appearance of civility which was all I wanted. We had pleasant weather with fair wind which brought us in four days to Fort Erie where to my great joy I got rid of my ladies. I staid at Fort Erie till the fourth of July, as I was ordered to bring up the rear and there was not bateaux to carry us all down to Fort Schlosser. During my stay, I lived with my old friends, the 65th, who had a port here, and was much obliged to them for their great civility. An Indian congress was held a few miles distant but I could not go to see it—it was on account of a tract of land that the Americans wished to purchase of the Indians, but the savages were averse to disposing of it. We left Fort Erie at four o'clock in the evening, and after having received a good drenching from a thunderstorm got safe to Fort Schlosser at sunset. I could not help observing the great improvement in the farms from what they were at our going up two years ago. On the 5th July I rose at daybreak and went to the falls of Niagara, but mistaking the path I was for some time in a swampy wood which I could not get through, and was obliged to come back and make a circuit of 7 miles instead of two. As I only saw it on the same side as I did before I shall not repeat the grandeur

July

of the scene; my time being again limited I left it with regret. At eleven o'clock in the morning I arrived with my detachment at the Landing and joined the Regt, who were waiting for bateaux to carry the baggage to Niagara where the Seneca was waiting to receive us. On the 6th, our baggage being all off, we marched to Niagara where we stay'd for the day and dined with the first Battalion of the 60th Regt. On the 7th sailed from Niagara and had the most pleasant weather possible —on the 9th we fell in with some islands in a fog which retarded us some time but the fog clearing we arriv'd in the evening (at Carleton Island)—the 10th drawing provision detained us some time, but we were all off by twelve o'clock and having a strong breeze we made such good use of our oars and sails that we went twenty leagues before we put up. We had fifteen boats and it was pretty to see such a fleet amongst the islands with which this part of the lake abounds. We lay on an island in order to keep the men from straggling amongst the settlers, who have now almost taken up the whole side of the lake and River from Coteau du Lac (where the Canadians end) to the Bay of Quinte—a tract of ⟨200⟩ miles. On the 11th we were early on board our boats and having passed the old fort of Oswegatchie, and the ruins of Fort Wm Augustus, entered the rapids. We went with astonishing rapidity down the first and second, without any difficulty, as our pilots were well informed of the proper channels, the only danger being in crossing the river, which you are obliged to do two or three times to avoid the rocks; but these were nothing to the third, called the Long Sault—it is nine miles long, and divided by islands into several channels, some of which, if you enter, inevitable destruction is the consequence. For the first five miles we were quite silent, with a swift current, which carried us on at a good gallop. The descent then became very visible, and the water rose in waves; but at last, on turning a point, we had the view of a stormy sea, with rocks and currents in every direction, and had a steep declivity to go down—we had scarcely time to think before we were hurried into it, and after a good struggle, and half drowned with the water that broke over us, we got through. We went these nine miles in twenty eight minutes, and soon after put up for the night; our days work was about 25 leagues and rain all the time, which made the boats very uncomfortable. It is astonishing to see the great improvements made by the Loyalists since our passing this way two years ago—good substantial houses have been built—the lands cleared to a good distance from the river—fields inclosed —a number of mills erected; and, in short, from the rude state in which we then saw it this part is now become one of the first settlements in Canada. As this is the season for muskitoes and sand-flies we are tormented by them perpetually, but of all the places I ever was at for muskitoes the Landing near Niagara is the first not only for numbers but size. The 12th we were off by daybreak and went three leagues to Lake St François. When we were about half way across we met four bateaux with recruits going to join the 65th Regiment; we just spoke to them and pursued our route down the rapids of Coteau du Lac, which we passed safely and, arriving at the Cedars, the greatest part of our men were landed and marched to the Cascades—6 miles. Some additional Canadians were put in each boat as these rapids are the most dangerous of any in the River St Lawrence, particularly a place called the Trou, where there appears a chasm in the bed of the river, and the waters rush down on one side, and rise over the other, in an extraordinary manner. They must have been bold fellows who first attempted it, as the only place that boats can pass it is very narrow, and any fault in the steering would be attended with certain death. On our march we saw the field where Major Forster[1] with a party of Indians and a few men of the Eighth defeated a body of the Americans, at the commencement of the Rebellion, and took some hundreds of them prisoners. We lay at the foot of the Cascades on a bank covered with wild rasberries, which was a good treat as there are none to be had at Detroit; they are the same sort as what grow in our gardens and are equally good when not spoilt by an insect that in going over them gives them the smell and taste of a bug. Some merchants who were going up with goods to Niagara and Detroit lay where we did and treated us with porter, which was to us a rarity—what we got at Detroit being in general horrid trash.

13th left the Cascades at 7 o'clock and had a most agreeable sail to La Chine, the day being fine, and the prospects on the Isle Jésu and the neighbourhood the most beautiful that can be imagin'd. At La Chine we landed and marched into Montreal, leaving our boats to the care of Canadians, who brought them down the rapids without any accident though they declared at first that they were so much loaded that they would not take charge of them. We arrived at Montreal about 6 o'clock in the evening and as we had provisions to draw were obliged to stay for the night, contrary to our intention. We received orders to leave some officers here for a General Court

[1] Two happenings in May 1776 combined to persuade the American invaders of Canada to retire. One was the arrival of reinforcements (which included Hughes's regiment) from England; the other the surprising success of Captain Forster, commander of the British post at Ogdensburg, in capturing 500 Americans with a small raiding party. (See note on p. 2.)

Martial—we left a captain and a subaltern, and after a good night's rest at the tavern kept by Sullivan, which was what we had not had since we left Detroit, got into our boats again about 8 o'clock on the 14th, and went 12 leagues. We put up early as it was a rainy day; we lay in Canadian houses and our men in barns. On the 15th we passed through Lake St Pierre, and not liking to trust our men in Trois Rivières, we just went a league beyond it, and lay in Canadian houses and barns as we did the night before. Trois Rivières, so called from three rivers that disembogue into the St Lawrence close by the town, is a large town, ill built and little or no trade; it is remarkable for the attack made by the Americans under General Thompson,[1] on the advance of General Carleton's army in the year 1776. Our jaunt this day was 19 leagues, but as we have now the tide to encounter, we must not expect to get on so fast.

JULY 15TH. Went off at daylight, and being favored by a small breeze got to Pointe aux Trembles, 22 leagues; we had a hard struggle with the tide for the last two hours—when the wind failed us. We passed several ships that were waiting for a wind to go to Montreal, and had a very agreeable voyage, as no river in the world can afford finer scenes than this part of the St Lawrence, which is in many parts three or four miles wide. Our men lay by their boats and the officers in Canadian houses.

JULY 16TH. The tide did not answer till eight o'clock—at eleven we put into Wolfe's Cove about 2 miles from Quebec just to let the men dress themselves, and about one we landed at the lower town and marched up to the blockhouses on Cape

[1] This incident is related, p. 5. Thompson attempted to recover Three Rivers.

Diamond where we are to remain till the barracks are repaired. I was surprised to see the number of ships in the harbour; there were at least thirty, which is a proof that the trade of the province must have greatly increased since our leaving this place in 1786, at which time we seldom had above five or six. Dined with the 26th Regiment, who are at present on duty here, but will leave it in a few days. We performed our journey in 19 days from Detroit to Quebec which is reckon'd 900 miles, not quite 50 miles a day one day with the other, which is no bad travelling for a body of men; indeed it is all downhill.

JULY 17TH. On the 17th we dined with the Artillery, and the next day were introduced to Lord Dorchester[1] with whom I dined at his country house. On my introduction to Lady Dorchester she scarcely deigned to move her head, but she is remarkable for her pride and ill breeding. Some time before I left Detroit I applied for leave to go home, and on my arrival at Quebec Major Mathews gave me great hopes of my wish being granted; but unfortunately for me, one of our gentlemen, who had a prior right, apply'd, and the major was obliged to tell me that I must remain with the Regt, as there are only ten subalterns with it which is just the King's Order. This is owing to the good nature of our colonel, who would not order the officers in England to join though many of them have been absent for five years. Soon after our arrival Lord Dorchester and Major Mathews went on a tour to the upper parts of the province—and on the 6th August the 28th Regt left us to go up the country.

AUGUST

Having now no great employment I shall amuse myself

[1] Sir Guy Carleton (see note on p. 2), who had been created a Baron in 1785, and reappointed Governor, 1786–96.

with throwing together what little intelligence I was able to get of the Indians during my stay at Detroit.

The Indians of North America differ greatly in their persons—though not in their complexions, which is copper colour, but they are in general so covered with grease and dirt that you seldom see their real skin—especially the northern nations such as the Esquimaux and Micmacs; the coldness of their climate has stinted their growth and there is as much difference between them and the more southern tribes as there is between a Laplander and an Englishman. As my knowledge of them was principally confined to the nations who border'd the Lakes, it is of them only I speak when I say that I never saw more complete figures for an artist to take models than the generality of the young warriors: their limbs are in the most perfect symmetry, their countenances open and their features good; they have all large black expressive eyes and black hair; the roman nose is common; and as for corpulency there's no such thing—which is extraordinary, as most of the children are pot bellied and as broad as they are long. Their size answers to the European, only that you seldom see a short or a very tall Indian; I never saw a man under five feet six inches, and very seldom above six feet—five feet nine and ten is the general run. The women are far from being so handsome as the men; they are low of stature, seldom above five feet six inches, oftener much less than more, and soon lose the little beauty they are bless'd with. Good teeth and very small feet are the only points of beauty that are lasting with them— indeed from the diminutive feet of the squaws one would be apt to imagine their mothers made use of some such means as the Chinese to prevent their growth, but with them it is pure nature.

The young Indians before they can walk are placed by their mothers with their backs against a board with a small flat place for their feet; they have a hoop, or some kind of binding which goes under their arms and fastens them to the board. In this situation they are carried by the mother at her back, and when she goes into a hut or house she generally hangs them on the outside on any thing that offers. Their growth is nowhere stopt by ligaments, and exposed as they are from their birth to all the variety of the seasons, their bodies become inured to the weather, which never affects them afterwards, and their limbs take the proper form that nature designed them. From these causes it is that we seldom meet either illness or deformity amongst this race of beings. As soon as the limbs are a little settled and have gain'd strength sufficient to crawl, the young savage is taken from the board and permitted to follow his own whims, care being taken to give him plenty of food and to prevent as much as possible his crying, by indulging him in every thing. By the time they are six or seven years, nothing can be imagined so completely fat; big bellies, broad faces, and the most astonishing sized legs and arms that can be imagined for such an age.

A different line of life then takes place; they begin to learn what may be called their exercises, running, shooting, canoeing and harpooning fish—not that they have schools for any thing of this kind but they are encouraged to it by their mothers and the desire of emulation. All their plays tend to make them active; in a short time they grow out of their fat, and by the age of ten or eleven become slim lads and as fleet as stags. They are then taught to despise dangers, to circumvent an enemy by taking every advantage and to suffer hardships, an idea of all which is given them in their dances or in the war songs; the smaller kind of hunting is likewise of use to harden them for greater undertakings. They then begin to associate with young men of their own age and by fifteen entirely discard all authority of the mother—and only wish for opportunities to signalise themselves either at the chase or on their enemies.

This is the education of the men; the women have a different line of breeding. Like the boys they are indulged in every thing till six or seven years old, when they are taught by their mothers the little works they know and are obliged to assist them in the necessary labour of the family. The squaws are the slaves; every thing that is wanted in the hut is their province. They are obliged to till the fields, hoe and gather the corn, dress the skins of the game, make moccasins, and if permitted to go with their husbands must carry the baggage— it would be a disgrace to a warrior to assist in any of these things, and no life can be more idle than that of a savage whilst at home with his family. He either is employed in mending or preparing some of his arms or tackle, or otherwise smoking and looking with the utmost tranquillity at the labour of the squaws, who in the harvest are obliged to work like horses. Another favourite way of passing their time is laying at full length on the grass and observing the young boys at play. This life they will lead for a length of time till roused by hunger, revenge, or the hunting season.

Every nation has a particular tract of country belonging to it called its hunting ground and which no other tribe is permitted to go upon—and almost all Indian wars arise from disputes about these lands, which being nothing but vast wildernesses, the haunt of different beasts, no wonder if the huntsmen led by plenty of game, or perhaps ignorance of the boundaries, often intrude on what belongs to others. Should he be met by the proprietors, an action immediately insues, and the blood spilt producing war—as nothing will satisfy the relations of the deceased but the blood of the adverse tribe, it does not matter whether it is the person that did the action or not.

The Indians have generally fixt residences where they raise their corn and may be called their homes; these may sometimes change either for the conveniency of being nearer their hunting grounds or because the lands are not good, or to place at a more secure situation from their enemies their wives and families. In these places, which we call villages, they generally build their huts near each other, and the fields cleared round about are in common to the whole. Here the wives and children remain whilst the husbands go to war or the hunt—and it is here in a hut set apart that they hold their councils and settle the concerns of the community.

It is not easy to define the Indian form of government, for though they have no hereditary chiefs yet they have families that are more respected than others, and it is from these families that their head men are generally chosen. The same honour may arrive to any Indian, but he must have signalised himself either at war or by his oratory—eloquence is the most certain road to fame, and those Indians who speak the best are always sent on their embassies, and generally bring the others to their mode of thinking at their conferences, or publick councils.

When an Indian goes to settle a treaty between his nation and any other, he always carries some strings of wampum which are larger or less according to the importance of the affair (the wampum string is a kind of beads cut out of a shell, which being strung together are ornamented with ribbons—

these are much esteemed and are accounted national riches). When he has made his speech, he gives the wampum which he held in his hand, and the people who receive it, keep it, to remind them of the subject; and their memories are so good that when they give their answer, tho' some time afterwards, they always repeat what has been said to them to shew that they have not forgot the least circumstance. The Indian language is by no means copious, which may be the reason that they make use of figurative expressions in their speeches and always accompany it with a great deal of action. When the ambassador comes to make peace, he first of all wipes the tears from your eyes, that you may no longer lament your killed, he then cleanses them from the dust that you may see your real friends; the path is opened and cleared of those obstructions that prevented your travelling, the hatchet is buried, and the chair of friendship brightened—these and such like expressions adapted to the subject are always made use of. If the peace is accepted of they all smoke out of the same pipe and the affair is soon concluded.

Some Indians declare war by sending a warrior to the boundaries of the other nation, who bids them defiance, and having thrown a dart into their land returns, on which the war dance is begun and those who choose to go enlist themselves, take up the hatchet, and after eating some of the meat that is cooked on the occasion—which is generally a dog— they set off, to surprise and destroy their enemies. If they are successful in their enterprise, they immediately return, with their scalps, prisoners, and booty, and seldom or never attempt a second stroke, whatever opening the disorder of their enemy, from this unexpected attack, may give them. On their way back they generally draw on some conspicuous tree an account of their expedition; it would be hard for an European to understand it, but an Indian on seeing these hieroglyphicks will tell you what nations were engaged, the number of warriors on each side, with the scalps, prisoners &c taken. They halt a small distance from their villages in order to dress and paint themselves and their prisoners; those captives that are doom'd to be burnt are painted black—the others red. When they begin their march, they give the war hoop to inform their friends of their arrival, and after that by particular cries they tell the success, and loss of the expedition; the whole village are by this means acquainted with every thing before they see their friends, and the squaws prepare themselves to receive the prisoners, on whom they exercise all manner of cruelties, especially those who have lost relations—sometimes prisoners are killed by these females before they can arrive at their appointed huts and very few escape mutilation. This ordeal over, those prisoners that are to be sacrificed are told to prepare themselves—the others are given to those that have lost relations, and if they adopt them, are immediately treated as one of themselves, and enter into all the rights of the person they replace, be it husband, brother, son, no matter which. What is remarkable, these adopted people espouse the interest of the new nation, fight against their own tribe, and if taken are treated in every respect as they would treat any other enemy.

In the mean time the poor victim, when informed of his fate, only says I thank you, and prepares himself by recalling to his memory all his war achievements, particularly those that he has performed against the nation with whom he is prisoner; these are to embellish his death song. Till he is brought to the stake, every want is supplied and every indulgence granted him. When led out, he walks undaunted, appears to look with unconcern at the faggots and display of implements with which he is to be tortur'd, and disdains to notice the scoffs and abuse of the bystanders. He is then tied to the post, and the pile, which is only near enough to scorch but not burn him, is lighted. The work of death then begins; every torture—every torment that human nature can devise—is made use of, and if they do not pursue any devilish invention that they have begun, it is not from compassion, but the fear of hastening the end of their entertainment, by exercising greater cruelties than mortal strength can bear. The warrior during this scene tells them first who he is, and the great names of his ancestors, then his own exploits, what numbers of his enemies he has scalped or taken, and at last describes to them how he tormented their relations, at such and such places, when like himself they were put to death; invectives succeed which generally bring on the final blow, as some of the executioners, hurt by his reproaches of cowardice &c, in a fit of frenzy give him a stroke of the tomahawk, but this seldom happens till they have exhausted their tortures and the strength of the prisoner almost gone.

These executions have been known to last several hours. When dead, they sometimes eat the body, either in soup or roasted, but this is not done from a like to human flesh, but out of a kind of bravado, and an idea that it will make them bolder; something of their religious tenets is likewise mixt in this practice, and savages have been known to suck the blood of their enemies in time of action for the same cause—and not from a delight in human flesh with which many have taxed them. No instance ever was known of an Indian of North America (or at least the parts we are acquainted with) ever eating a prisoner but on such an occasion as is above described, and they seldom then do more than taste the flesh—except indeed a young fellow who wishes to appear bolder than his comrades.

When a party of Indians have undertaken an expedition, whether against their enemies or merely for the purpose of hunting, no obstacles can stop them; hunger, thirst, inclemency of the season, and every other ill they suffer without murmuring, and steadily pursue their route through the trackless wildernesses with astonishing precision, almost always making the very place they wish to arrive at—though distant several hundred miles from their own villages. The sun, when the woods will permit the seeing him, is their compass, but when that fails they are not at a loss, and will keep going to the same point with little or no variation; the growth of the trees, the course of the waters, and other signs which they know direct them in their journey.

The Indians' travelling dress is a pair of moccasins or shoes, a pair of cloth leggings which come half way up his thighs, a breech clout and a blanket—these, with his fire-arms and a small quantity of Indian corn, compose his whole stock of baggage. They seldom stop during the day and if they take any refreshment it is never more than a small quantity of Indian meal mixt in the hollow of their hand with some water. At night they cook what they have killed in the day, make a wigwam or hut with branches of trees, and lie with their feet to the fire if in winter; and I have been assur'd by gentlemen who have gone on winter scouts that these sheds or huts are warm even in the coldest time. The Indians always dig the snow till they come to the ground, which as the snow is light is soon done with their snow shoes; all the snow is flung up against the quarter the wind blows from—but in the woods the wind is never very high, as it may blow a storm and you would know nothing of it but by the rustling of the branches. They then construct the hut under cover of the heap of snow —leaving it quite open towards the fire—and for a bed they cut fir and other winter trees, the small branches of which make a very good one. As the bed is below the level of the snow—and the heat of the fire retained by the slanting roof— the traveller finds a single blanket sufficient to lie comfortable. The Indians are so expert at this kind of camping that in half an hour after they have stopt for the day every thing is finished, and perhaps the pot—if they have any—is over the fire. Unless very near the enemy they have no fix'd guards in the night, but some of them are almost always up—or walking round the camp—so that it is difficult to surprise them; for being always dress'd and their arms lying by them—they are ready in an instant. They are the best of wood soldiers but will not stand in an open country.

Some of the southern Indians, such as the Sioux, Pawnees &c, fight on horseback with spears and bows and arrows—in their countries are vast plains or savannahs, where they chase the buffalo. Some of these savannahs are a hundred miles long, cover'd with grass four or five feet high, and abounding in buffaloes, who go in herds of some hundreds. The Pawnees are in a state of warfare with all the northern nation and they are the only nation that are sold—and sell—for slaves all that are taken prisoners. Many of them were at Detroit—bought of the Indians who had taken them. The Pawnees live on the south side of the Mississippi and are by all accounts a very numerous nation—they make bad slaves, being idle and always trying to get away.

Female virtue is very little thought of amongst the unmarried Indian girls, but when married they are very faithful. A father or brother will pimp for you—and think himself well paid with a bottle of rum—but a husband would stab both you and his wife were he to suspect an intimacy; but this jealousy of the wife is only from national custom, not from love, as is visible from the little attention paid by the men to their wives, who are in fact no better than their slaves and beasts of burden; and one nation to the north west—when they go to hunt—put the traders in possession of their houses and wives that they may be provided for during their absence. Such is the force of habit and prejudice—and might be brought home to the Europeans, with this difference, that brother and father will cut your throat and the husband be sometimes much obliged to you.

OCTOBER. At the return of Lord Dorchester from visiting the upper country, we were reviewed, but the season was so advanced that the men had scarcely the use of their fingers from the cold. We came off with as much credit as could be expected from the motley composition of our corps, which was made up of drafts and cast-off men from all the Regts that had left Canada for ten years before.

# 1789

The winter was as gay as balls, routs, and a variety of other amusements could make it. I entered pretty much into the general amusements, but my perpetual ailings prevented my enjoying them to any satisfaction, and the beginning of March, finding myself worse, I went into the country to a French house; but the living was so contrary to what I had been used to that I was obliged to come into town at the end of six weeks miserably reduced and new complaints which made me unhappy. At this time died Brig: Genl Hope,[1] the Lt Governor, entirely owing to the doctor mistaking his disorder, which was venereal—before his death he was a miserable object having lost eyes, nose, teeth &c, &c. He was much regretted and was a publick as well as a private loss—he upheld the Scotch party against the Yankee interests which was but too prevalent in all departments of Canadian government. His wife and niece, who had but just come out to stay with him, were reduced to low circumstances, and deserved much compassion. And shall I here mention your name, Letitia, best, softest of thy sex, and recall—no; bonds more firm than adamant retain thee and oblivion must efface thee from my remembrance. The 14th of May brought us a ship from England and on the 25th—Captain Houghton announced to me the death of my much honour'd, ever dear Mother. Words are inadequate to paint my feelings—in her I lost the tenderest of parents and the best of friends.

APRIL

MAY
25TH

[1] He had administered the Government of Quebec from November 1785 till Dorchester arrived in October 1786.

It was late in May before the snow left the face of the country—in the winter it had been five feet deep on a level which is more than was ever known before. The King's malady,[1] which had greatly distressed all the English subjects, was by the first ships announced to be cured. Illuminations and other demonstrations of joy testified the love of the people to the Sovereign—but this must be only understood of the English subjects, which indeed make great part of the population of the Province; the Canadians still look with fond regard to their old government, being too much attached to French customs and the Catholic religion ever to adopt the English interest, in which I am sorry to say their priests seem to encourage them, notwithstanding the favours they have received and the mildness with which they have been treated. The French standard if once erected in Canada would be crowded to by the common race of Canadians; for the better sort I am in hopes their good sense would shew them that their true interest was connected with the British—but of this I have my doubts. The common Canadians are very ignorant—not very religious, and yet the most foolishly credulous of any set of beings I ever met with. They are stout made fellows, dark complexioned, and cheerful dispositioned; active in their pleasure, but not much inclined to labour—except it is in rowing and managing boats which seems to be their element. They live dirtily and seldom make any improvements in the lands they receive from their fathers—which is the reason that the English settlers in the course of five or six years have JUNE already better farms than those Canadians who were settled before the conquest. At this time there is

[1] The first clear appearance of insanity in George III's condition, 1788–9.

almost a famine in the country, more corn having been permitted to have been exported last year than the country could afford to spare. Many families have been obliged to live on the bark of trees—some on boiled hay—and not enough corn to sow the ground this year—so that every thing is to be dreaded. It certainly was a great oversight to permit the exportation; but interested people deceived the governor—who I suppose was at the same time willing to shew the great advance the Province had made in point of cultivation and agriculture.

On the 18th of June Government despatches being receiv'd by Ld Dorchester, with ministerial accounts of the King's recovery, we had a feu de joie with bon fires, illuminations &c, &c. At this time I was completely laid up by an inflammation of the stomach brought on by indigestion; every thing was stop'd in my stomach—and had most violent convulsive spasms. My complaint continued without relief tho' I had the best advice, being that of Doctor Nooth.

On the 6th July the 24th Regt came from England to relieve us. A fever that had got amongst the ships' company prevented our going off so soon as we expected; we were reviewed the 21st—at which time I was so reduced from not being able to eat, drink or sleep that I had scarcely strength to walk 100 yards. I write this on the 23rd and am at present a skeleton, as I am really starving—my appetite is good but I dare not eat as it brings on convulsions. My days appear to me to be run, for which reason I have to return the Almighty God thanks for the life and benefits that I have enjoy'd; and as it is most probable I shall still hold out some days longer, and as I am to embark on the 30th of this month—which I am convinced will be my death or my being reduced so low that

I shall not be able to carry the Journal any farther—I thus sincerely take leave of all my dearest friends, wishing them every happiness in this life and that God will be pleased to let us meet in happiness in the next. Should any unforeseen turn in my disorder make me well again—as it must come only from God I here promise to make a gift of ten guineas to the poor, and if I omit it God will punish me as I deserve. My spirits are still good—I go off gradually nor shall my endeavours be wanting to bear up against the disorder. I beg God to give patience to bear what he is pleased to inflict, and that it may not be too severe but that my death like my life may be quiet and placid. My character is known to my friends—and to others it is of no consequence. I am far from being without faults—but I know of no very crying sins—and I trust in the goodness of God and the mediation of my Redeemer Jesus Christ to have them forgiven; to whom I now recommend myself this 23rd day of July 1789 being thirty years of age.

THOS. HUGHES

*Died the* 10th *January* 1790—*of consumption*

I.H.

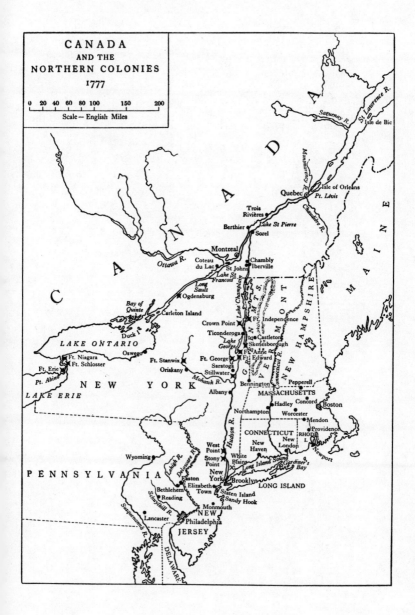

CANADA
AND THE
NORTHERN COLONIES
1777

0  20  40  60  80 100  150      200
Scale – English Miles